To the Board of Trustees and the Staff
of the American Indian Archaeological Institute
for their support
and
To all the participants
in the excavation and analysis
for their superb dedication and quality of work

ABOUT THE AUTHOR

Roger Moeller was born in Middletown, Connecticut, in 1945 and graduated from Franklin and Marshall College (A.B.) and the State University of New York at Buffalo (M.A., Ph.D.) with a major in Anthropology and a specialization in Archaeology. He conducted excavations at prehistoric sites in Central and Western New York, in the Susquehanna and Delaware Valleys of Pennsylvania, and in Western Connecticut.

Before becoming Director of Research at the AIAI, he taught at Millard Fillmore College, State University of New York at Buffalo, Dickinson College, and Franklin and Marshall College. In addition to his research duties he is teaching at The Gunnery School and in summer field programs with the University of Hartford, Fairfield University, and the Graduate Teachers' Center at Fairfield.

He has maintained a close contact with other archaeological organizations as business manager and president-elect of the Eastern States Archaeological Federation, treasurer of the Society for Pennsylvania Archaeology, and past secretary of the Archaeological Society of Connecticut.

6LF21

A PALEO-INDIAN SITE
IN WESTERN CONNECTICUT

ROGER W. MOELLER

OCCASIONAL PAPER NUMBER 2
AMERICAN INDIAN ARCHAEOLOGICAL INSTITUTE

WASHINGTON, CONNECTICUT

Library of Congress Catalog Number 80-65186
ISBN 0-89488-010-1

The publication of *6LF21: A Paleo-Indian Site in Western Connecticut* was made possible by a grant from **Reader's Digest,** and all proceeds from the sale of the book will be placed in a permanent endowment fund to assist in financing future publications of the Institute.

Printed in the United States of America by
SHIVER MOUNTAIN PRESS, INC.
Washington Depot, Connecticut 06794

CONTENTS

TABLES

FIGURES

PLATES

ACKNOWLEDGEMENTS

The excavation was conducted during a 12-week period in 1977 under the supervision of the Research Staff of the American Indian Archaeological Institute (AIAI): Dr. Russell G. Handsman, Dr. Roger W. Moeller, Roberta Hampton, and Stephen Post. Field mapping was coordinated by two other staff members, Jean Pruchnik and Sharon Wirt. Jean and Sharon cataloged the entire collection with the assistance of two dedicated volunteers, Jane French and Kay Schaller.

The diligent and capable excavation crew and laboratory assistants were members of field schools and training programs co-sponsored by the AIAI and The Gunnery School, University of Hartford, Fairfield University, Graduate Teachers' Center at Fairfield, Earthwatch and Center for Field Research of Belmont, Massachusetts. Without the continuing support of these institutions, the fieldwork and subsequent analysis could not have been done. They assisted in recruiting volunteers and students, raising funds, and generating interest in our excavations.

I would also like to thank Dr. Meyer Rubin of the U.S. Geological Survey Radiocarbon Laboratory, Reston, Virginia, for providing the radiocarbon date, as well as Dr. R. Bruce Hoadley, Wood Science and Technology, University of Massachusetts, Amherst, who arranged for one of his students, Karen Saunders, to identify wood charcoal samples.

All of the Figures were drawn by Jean Pruchnik. Myron Mack, Fairfield, Connecticut, was a professional photographer in insisting that his photographs of the artifacts were as clear and as sharp as possible. The cover design by Sharon Wirt and Jean includes Jean's original drawings, as well as photographs by Myron, Stephen Post, and the author. Additional photographic work was done by Lester Rich and Frederick Clymer.

I sincerely appreciate the helpful criticisms from all of the individuals who read summaries, drafts, and the final manuscript: John and Joan Brothers, Don Ethier, Myron Mack, Ruth Nalven, Ellis Settle, Kathleen Taylor, and Sharon Wirt. Ursula O'Donnell made a valiant effort in interpreting my hieroglyphics when she typed the first draft.

The founder and president of the AIAI, Edmund (Ned) Swigart, provided not only constant encouragement throughout the excavation, analysis, and writing, but also the freedom to work on this project to the exclusion of nearly all other duties. Ned also initiated the discussions leading to the funding of this publication by The Reader's Digest Foundation.

Last, but by far not least, my special thanks go to the landowners who permitted the excavation, but who shall remain anonymous to retain their privacy.

PREFACE

The primary function for a preface is to explain to the reader why the book was written and how the author intended it to be used. This preface will go beyond that to explain why the book does not follow the traditional format of most archaeological site reports.

The uniqueness of 6LF21 could not be discussed only at meetings of professional and amateur archaeologists or in their limited circulation journals. The coverage of the excavation and preliminary analysis in local, state, regional, and national newspapers, radio, and television stimulated a very high level of interest among the general public. The AIAI Research Department received hundreds of letters, phone calls, and visitors asking for more information. In response to that demand this site report has been written in a format understandable to the non-archaeologist.

The first chapter is a general summary of the procedures and results. Subsequent chapters provide more complete descriptions of the data, discussions of the logical steps followed in reaching conclusions, and references to the work of other researchers which substantiate these interpretations or suggest alternative hypotheses.

The Appendices contain the Tables, Figures, and Plates describing the artifacts and their distribution at the site. While for certain people this will necessitate flipping back and forth to examine the data referenced in the text, it will not interrupt the flow of the text for the average reader.

A very serious attempt has been made to avoid archaeological jargon in the body of the book, to invite the generally interested person to understand this site without having to take a course in archaeology or to constantly refer to other books for definitions of terms. Jargon does serve an important function whenever it is used.

People who speak the same jargon know more precisely what is meant. There are nuances of meaning which common words cannot convey. However, since the primary interest in this site has been heavily weighted towards the general public, that is the audience to which this book is addressed.

The technical jargon, statistical comparisons, and detailed tables have been put at the back of the book where they will not impede the flow of the text, but will still be accessible to the interested reader. Two of the questions most frequently asked of the archaeologist by the lay person are, "What was life like for the Indians before the Europeans came?" and "How do you know life was really like that?" Chapter One provides a summary of the procedures used in the excavation, of the analysis, and of the interpretation of the oldest dated site in Connecticut. Subsequent chapters explore each of the topics presented in greater detail.

Two explanations are in order so that the non-archaeologist can better understand what is happening. "6LF21" is archaeological shorthand for the 21st recorded site in Litchfield County, Connecticut. Connecticut is sixth in an alphabetical listing of the 48 states prior to the admission of Alaska and Hawaii. They were assigned 49 and 50 rather than renumber all of the previously cataloged sites and their artifacts.

Sites usually have a common name in addition to the number, especially if there are many sites in a small area. The common name may be the landowner's name or a geographical feature. In this case the number was used because the same family owned many plots of land on which were other sites.

"Paleo-Indian" is the term archaeologists use to refer to the people who were among the first to occupy the continental United States and Canada. While there are scattered clues to suggest that man first entered the New World more than 30,000 years before Paleo-Indian, these early people are very poorly known archaeologically. Paleo-Indian artifacts and sites have been studied in sufficient detail to permit many generalizations which were thought to be true under all circumstances, but can be seen as potentially deceptive stereotypes.

Although these groups lived about 10,000 years ago and their remains are commonly found between 12,000 and 7,000 years ago, there were many distinct subdivisions, regional adaptations, and types of artifacts. The supposed diagnostic artifact, the fluted point—named for its medial groove (see Plate 7), is found only among the early groups. Later Paleo-Indian groups had non-fluted points.

Paleo-Indian has been stereotyped as the Big Game Hunter, as though he ate only mammoth, mastodon, caribou, and bison, but recent excavations in Pennsylvania have shown that he ate fish, as well as fruit and seeds. Since he lived more than 10,000 years ago in areas of the East which were then just recently deglaciated, he was stereotyped as surviving with the bare essentials in a tundra environment. Subsequent pollen studies modified this to a pine-spruce forest. Current research is yielding evidence that the actual sites of human habitation were more likely to have included deciduous trees, not just evergreens.

Subsequent chapters will discuss the real Paleo-Indian based upon direct observations and not stereotypes. Dates, diagnostic artifacts, food remains, and environmental reconstruction are discussed for 6LF21 and nearby sites.

The general reader without previous archaeological experience should first look at the Figures and Plates to become acquainted with the small amount of archaeological jargon used in this book (Fig. 11) and with the 10,000-year-old artifacts which were found at the site. From the pictures the next step should be to read the first chapter. I expect that most people will then skip to those sections of the book which were of greatest interest in the first chapter. Others will continue to read the text in sequence to follow the full story as it unfolds.

CHAPTER ONE

What would you give to be the first person to see something that had been made by man and had been hidden for 10,000 years? What would be your reaction to having participated in the discovery of these items, being told that they were incredibly unique and important, and then being sworn to secrecy? This was the situation for 110 participants in the excavation of 6LF21 during the summer of 1977. Most of the people had never before participated in or even visited a real archaeological site, but they were uncovering what was to become the oldest dated site in Connecticut and one of the most important ones of that age in the entire Eastern United States. How were these lucky few selected? How did they know where to dig? The story begins in 1969.

Edmund (Ned) Swigart of Washington, Connecticut became so interested in the prehistory of Western Connecticut that he formed the Shepaug Valley Archaeological Society (SVAS) to discover, preserve, and interpret the lifeways of the earliest inhabitants of New England. In the following years the society grew in membership and stature as the members uncovered more and more information in an area which had not seen systematic archaeological work. One of their continuing projects was the mapping of local sites and cataloging of collections.

One of the people who approached the SVAS with artifacts he had collected over years of gardening in his front yard was a co-owner of 6LF21. The artifacts he had were about 4,000 years old, but the context from which they came was more intriguing than their age.

In 1973 Ned Swigart and Donald Engelman, a student from The Gunnery School, a local boarding school, dug several test pits where the other artifacts had been found. While these test pits did not reveal evidence of a Paleo-Indian occupation, a hearth in one was carbon-14 dated to 2100 B.C. At the time this was the oldest dated site in Connecticut.

As the SVAS continued to grow, the need arose for a museum

1

facility staffed by professionals who could coordinate archaeological excavation, analysis, and interpretation; artifact storage; and the dissemination of the organization's findings to the general public, as well as the archaeological professionals. At this point it was renamed the American Indian Archaeological Institute (AIAI) to reflect its more diverse goals and scope of interest.

One of the most important and well-attended events during every summer since the formation of the SVAS was the excavation program. In previous years this had been a volunteer affair with an uncertain number of participants with varying degrees of expertise and motivation. But, by 1976 a series of formal field schools and training programs had been introduced, and in 1977 the plan was to increase the number of participants and run several two-week programs, one-week programs for college credit, and one-week training sessions. Because of the ambitious nature of an excavation program planned to last 10 weeks, an appropriate site had to be selected.

In addition to being able to accommodate between 10 and 25 workers at one time, the site also had to have the potential for providing information not already known about the local area. It would have been foolish to have wasted a lot of time on a site which was scientifically meaningless. Since one of the goals of the AIAI and its predecessor, SVAS, was to determine the culture history of the Shepaug Valley and to determine its relationship to that of adjacent areas, we were looking for a site having evidence of many different cultures which could be excavated in sequential order. Such stratified sites had been found in all areas where extensive excavations have been made except for the Shepaug Valley.

The advantage of stratification is that each occupation which has occurred at the site is vertically separated from the previous and subsequent ones. Since many different occupations are seen without mixture from other groups, the archaeologist is able not only to see what one group was doing at one time, but also what previous and subsequent groups did in the same area at different times.

This is why 6LF21 was considered. The surface collection and the artifacts found in the test pits showed that the site had been repeatedly occupied for at least 4,000 years. While the vertical separation of the artifacts was not apparent in the test pits, the amount of fine-grained sand in the pits suggested that some area within the field may have similar artifacts in a better context.

The fine-grained sand was deposited during very gradual flooding of the site. Had the flooding been severe enough to have disturbed or even washed away the artifacts left behind by various inhabitants, the soil would have been much coarser in texture. Also, the depth of the fine-grained soil was much greater here than other places previously excavated in the Shepaug Valley, thus increasing the potential vertical separation between successive encampments. All of this was theoretically very encouraging, but only more testing would reveal the truth of the suppositions.

In the spring of 1977 The Gunnery Afternoon Archaeology Program students directed by the author began a concentrated preliminary study of 6LF21. Because of geological factors discussed in more detail below, a section of the site near the confluence of the river and a small stream was cleared. The soil was at least 1.5m (5 feet) deep and very fine grained with few stones. Sifting of topsoil showed a mixture of tools ranging in age from modern times to 1000 B.C. All of these items in the topsoil had been churned by plowing and were out of context.

Immediately below the plow zone diagnostic artifacts nearly 3,500 years old were found *in situ* and in quantity. Deeper excavation revealed more artifacts of earlier times. We had found what had been predicted and long hoped for: a stratified site having numerous artifacts of different groups which were vertically separated. The decision was made to spend several weeks expanding this test excavation using field school students.

Students came from all over the United States and Canada to spend a week or two learning about archaeological excavation, analysis, and interpretation at a real site. When the unique nature of the site became apparent after the third week of excavation, the students and staff were warned not to discuss their findings. While most archaeological work is done in the open and visitation is encouraged, we were concerned that the spectacular nature of this site might raise too much interest. This could lead to unauthorized digging (pothunting), visitation when we were not there to prevent damage, and premature publicity preventing us from working undisturbed.

The precautions were well-advised since all of these dire scenarios occurred within one week of the public announcement of the finds. Since the announcement had been delayed until the last weeks of the excavation, after nearly all of the data had been gathered, the damage and disruptions from pothunters, tourists, and media were minimal. But this is getting ahead of the story.

The finding of the Paleo-Indian artifacts nearly 1.5m (5 feet) below the surface came as a tremendous surprise. The first clue that there was actually something cultural at that depth was flint chips. The use of flint in the Shepaug Valley was limited to relatively recent inhabitants, others about 3,000 years ago, and Paleo-Indian. Since we had already found evidence of the first two at higher levels, this meant either Paleo-Indian or another group not previously known

3

archaeologically for its use of flint. The flint chips were simply by-products of stone tool manufacture and were not diagnostic in themselves. However, this clue prompted the excavation of adjacent squares to the same depth. Adjacent squares had the same kind of flint chips in the same association. They were being found in the band of clay-coated sand which had been deposited over a bed of cobbles, which was initially interpreted as being part of a glacial deposit, thus "confirming" the date of these chips as being just after the last glacier had receded more than 12,000 years ago.

It was not until the fluted point was found that this level could be assigned to Paleo-Indian times, between 12,000 and 10,000 years ago. The excavation plan stayed the same and adjacent squares were excavated to the cobble layer. By the time the excavation was completed, an estimated 90% of the entire camp had been uncovered revealing more than 7400 artifacts in a 42.75m² (461 ft²) area.

After an excavation lasting 12 weeks, the analysis took nearly two years to complete. During this period, every single artifact was examined several times for evidence of utilization or deliberate chipping to make a functional implement. The nature and location of the manufacturing debris were quantified and recorded. Relationships between and among the various types of data from the site were examined.

Tools identified from the Paleo-Indian occupation were graving spurs, gravers, drills, spokeshaves, scrapers, fluted point, miniature points, hammerstone, and knives. In addition were unfinished tools which had been rejected prior to completion, tools of unknown function, and specialized lithic debris typical of Paleo-Indian manufacturing techniques: bifacial thinning flakes and channel flakes.

Graving spurs have a sharp point and edge to pierce soft materials and then slit them. Gravers have a more substantial point for piercing, with beveled sides for cutting and wedging a hole into more resistant materials. The drill is a third pointed implement used similarly to its modern counterpart.

Spokeshaves are specialized scrapers for preparing cylindrical wooden (spear) shafts. Other scrapers may have been used for working hides of animals killed by the fluted points. The miniature points do resemble the fluted point in overall appearance, but their function is unknown. Possibly they were ceremonial replicas or even toys.

The hammerstone is an all-purpose implement used in stone tool manufacture, food processing, bone crushing, and for many other functions requiring heavy pounding. The unfinished tools, bifacial thinning flakes, channel flakes, and waste flakes show the manufacturing sequence and reinforce the idea that no one is perfect. Even the skilled stone craftsmen made mistakes and produced a lot of debris relative to the number of finished artifacts.

Some charcoal from the site was carbon-14 dated. A small sample from a possible remnant of a prehistoric post was dated to 10,190 years ago (8240 B.C.). Since the sample was taken from the level at which all of the Paleo-Indian artifacts had been found, and many were actually found very close to where the sample was taken, the date of the charcoal applies to the age of all the Paleo-Indian artifacts. The date for Paleo-Indian came as no surprise since all of the sites with similar artifacts in the Northeast and, in general, the rest of the Eastern United States (Fig. 1) are approximately the same age.

The biggest surprise came when other charcoal samples were submitted for identification of the tree species from which they came. The samples submitted from the Paleo-Indian level were from red oak and either juniper or white cedar. Until this excavation, the environment in the Northeast at this time was thought to have been that of a pine-spruce forest which had emerged after the glacier had melted. The fact that these people were burning red oak and either juniper or white cedar changes this environmental picture in important ways.

Although the dominant tree species may well have been pine and spruce, the presence of red oak clearly shows a more diverse environment then thought previously. Since deciduous trees such as red oak are commonly found associated with florally and faunally more diverse environments than are evergreens, the implication is that anyone living in such an environment would be better able to survive. Rather than depend upon a relatively few plants and animals in an evergreen forest, man could increase his chances for survival by inhabiting areas with deciduous trees.

Since there is scant evidence that man was living in the Northeast in a tundra (open grasslands) or even a taiga (coniferous evergreen) forest, the potential significance of mammoth and mastodon in Paleo-Indian's diet is decreased. These beasts could have survived until the time of man's occupation, but are not as likely to be found in a dense forest. The prevalent stereotype of man, the big game hunter, during this period is subject to debate with this new environmental evidence.

Actually, the evidence is not completely new. Oak and other deciduous trees have been identified from sites of this age and earlier in Pennsylvania. They were either dismissed as possibly intrusive contaminants from subsequent occupations or the data had not yet reached the majority of archaeologists concerned with environmental reconstructions and their implications.

Not only can the denseness of the forest cover and types of likely companion trees and animals be hypothesized from the presence of red oak and juniper or white cedar, but also the general type of climate. These trees are likely to be found in a relatively warm, moist environment which has temperature fluctuations no more severe than that of modern-day southern Canada.

One of the most important conclusions reached was that this excavation revealed undisturbed evidence of life as it existed 10,000 years ago. The lack of significant disturbance is suggested by the artifacts being found only within a narrow band of clay-coated sand. This sandy band showed no evidence of erosional channels even though the cobble layer slopes very steeply towards the river. The possibility of sheet wash removing a thin layer of dirt over the entire area and thus disturbing the original positions of the artifacts was discounted in two ways. First, the tiny flakes of stone are not clustered in one area as though they had been washed to the lowest point of the site. Second, the finding of fitting fragments of artifacts only slightly displaced from one another shows that a lot of post-depositional horizontal movement is not likely to have occurred.

On the other hand, vertical movement of artifacts has almost definitely occurred. As one digs deeper into the levels within a given square, the frequency of artifacts increases until a maximum is reached, then the number declines. This is likely to occur only by the settling or rising of the specimens due to natural forces such as frost action, dry-wet cycles, or even minor insect burrowing.

Looking at the artifacts within a single square and its many levels, one will see a very high correlation between the general manufacturing debris (stone chips) and the more specialized debris from the manufacture of certain types of tools (bifacial thinning flakes) with the spent artifacts located nearby. This is not likely to happen by accident. The interpretation of these data is as follows: large chunks of stone were being worked to nearly the finished stage. Some of the nearly finished ones were flaked bifacially to make specific types of artifacts for immediate use. The artifacts were then used right where they had been manufactured. The ones found were discarded as they became useless for their designated functions.

Since it is uncommon to find so much manufacturing debris with so many spent tools in such a small area, more questions were raised. From where did the stone come that they were working? Since it is unlikely that they would transport unworked stone a great distance, a local source was sought. The best clue to the nature of the local source was the water-polished exterior of some of the waste flakes which had sharp edges. A search of the banks of the Shepaug River during the summer of 1977 revealed several small cobbles of flint similar to those flakes found on the site. Using this clue that the flint may have been available adjacent to the site, we felt that the presence

6

of the quantity of chippage on the site was more reasonably explained. A search later revealed a possible origin for that flint about three miles upstream of the site.

A second question raised concerned the duration of the occupation. Despite the huge quantity of chippage excavated with the artifacts, the original weight of the stone chunks need not have totaled more than 2.7 kg (6 lbs). This is not very much stone and could have been worked by a small group of people in less than one day. The degree of wear evidenced on the discarded artifacts need not have taken more than a few days to have occurred. Even considering the number of possible functions for which the artifacts may have been used one need not have done much more than butcher a single large animal, scrape the hide, make a few bone implements, and prepare for further hunting while another member of the group processed food for immediate consumption and for a few days' supply after the camp was abandoned.

With a total excavated area of less than 43m² and a probable total area of occupation of less than 50m², the camp could not have been occupied by very many people or for very long. If this were more than a short-term camp, the area over which the artifacts were scattered should have been larger and there should have been evidence of hearths.

With a very short-term occupation by a small group for a specialized function such as hunting, one would not expect quite such a diversity of artifacts to be used or for them to have been manufactured on the spot. This is a dilemma because, on one hand, the diversity of remains found is usually thought to be indicative of a long-term base camp in which many activities were being performed at a single time. But, hunting camps would not be expected to have so much manufacturing debris. What could be present at this site is an unexpectedly short-term camp in which the usual base camp features are present, but which had to be abandoned before the normal accumulation of debris had occurred.

When compared to other Paleo-Indian sites in the Eastern United States, 6LF21 can be said to be unique. Although the date of the site and the variety of artifacts found are typical of Paleo-Indian sites, the undisturbed nature of the data is remarkable. It is even more remarkable that this site was occupied only once. The possibility of multiple overlapping occupations in the area excavated is so small as to be nearly impossible. The artifacts of a single type are too similar in their manufacture and the nature of their working edges for different groups to have made them. The association of manufacturing debris with bifacial thinning flakes and discarded artifacts is too precise to have been accidental or to have been deposited by different

7

groups. Even the gradual increase in the number of artifacts in each level to a maximum point and then a decline in the same level throughout the entire site is too consistent to have been a result of different groups' debris accumulating over the centuries. Everything points to a single, short-term encampment.

If this is the case, then archaeologists have a unique opportunity to define the components of a single tool kit, and also the limits of the variability in man's tool kit at a single point in time. The manufacturing debris and the tools broken during manufacture show most precisely the expertise of a single group or even a single individual.

The quality of the data is so high because the site had never been disturbed by significant natural or cultural forces after it was abandoned. The excavation occurred during a relatively short period of time under the same supervision using the same techniques throughout. This is the exception rather than the rule at most Paleo-Indian sites which have yielded numerous artifacts in good association. The data from this site also have far-reaching ramifications for all Paleo-Indian research.

The environmental data not only reinforce what has been hinted at in previous excavations but, because of the near absence of disturbance, add substantial credulity to the interpretation of past climate and econiches actually occupied by man. Archaeologists had long relied upon pollen samples drawn from bogs for environmental reconstructions. These data are of the general environment, not the environment where man was actually living. The differences had never been thought to be significant before this investigation. This should prompt a rethinking of that position and lead others to more environmental data actually gleaned from where man was living and not where the preservation may be better.

As the data and the circumstances from which they are collected improve, so shall the interpretations. The stereotypes perpetuated by the data of the 1950's depicting the hide-clad nomads trekking across the trackless and treeless snow-covered plains in search of their next mastodon must be destroyed. Man cannot live by mastodon alone, nor would he have wanted to depend upon any single food source.

Any interpretations of environment 10,000 years ago must now take into consideration a deciduous element in addition to the conifers. The food potential of this environment coupled with carbonized seeds and fish bones actually recovered at other sites add clues to the possible diet of the people.

The similarities inherent in the spatially separated sites of this time period permit the application of data from one to the others, but these data initially must be applied tentatively lest existing conflicts be ignored. When the data do not conflict, the theoretical possibilities are enhanced for all sites of this period. Previously unreported data which were thought to be meaningless may surface because of the finds at 6LF21.

As in all excavations, this one has yielded information of theoretical importance to all archaeologists, not only those working with Paleo-Indian. One of the most important lessons was that this site was in the "wrong" place. Until this excavation, Paleo-Indian sites had not been found deeply buried on the floodplains of minor rivers. This seeming contradiction to the established pattern of where these sites "should" be is not really a contradiction but a flaw in archaeological reasoning.

The only reason that Paleo-Indian sites were found in specific locales is that that was where everyone was looking for them. The reason they were not sought in other settings is that they had not been found there. Using the established pattern of looking for Paleo-Indian sites in areas where they were previously found would lead one only to those sites which had been disturbed by erosion, open to view, and then disturbed by recent man.

The reason that sites were not found previously in a deeply-buried floodplain is that no one was digging there to find them. If they were not exposed (and therefore, disturbed), then they were not found. Although the finding of such a tiny camp in that huge field may have been luck, the pattern of where people should be looking for the best sites cannot be denied.

The purpose of this brief introductory statement was to pique the interest and to provide an abstract for the rest of the book. I have also attempted to provide the reader with an insight into the procedures used and the significance of the findings.

SITE SELECTION

The site was first brought to the attention of Edmund Swigart, president and founder of the AIAI, nearly 10 years ago by the landowners. The diversity of projectile point types in their surface collection from plowed fields indicated a series of occupations by many different groups ranging in age from only a few hundred to a few thousand years ago.

Under the supervision of Edmund Swigart, Donald Engelman, a student at The Gunnery School, conducted test excavations in 1973. His five 5 x 5 foot test pits were dug approximately 1m deep in different sections of the field. He carefully sifted the dirt from each test pit and recorded his findings.

Despite the incredibly tiny percentage of the total area of the field tested and the small size of each test pit, Engelman's assessment of the remarkable importance of this site was absolutely correct for all of the wrong reasons. His field notes show he appreciated the significance of the contrasting soil layers separating different types of artifacts. Since the material he was finding was primarily Archaic, which is thousands of years more recent than Paleo-Indian, the excellent context would be likely to yield a series of well-separated occupations. Since the Archaic is very poorly understood in Connecticut because single occupation sites are rare or unrecognized, the possibility of having one to analyze was enticing.

Because no one was looking for a Paleo-Indian site and the excavators did not have any experience with Paleo-Indian artifacts other than fluted points, a tiny clue was miscataloged and lay unnoticed for seven years in an envelope in a box in an artifact storage cabinet. It was not until this book was being prepared that a reanalysis of all the material ever found at the site uncovered an envelope labeled "Flint Chips". Among the stone chips was a thumbnail scraper (Plate 11b). While this is not a perfectly diagnostic Paleo-Indian artifact, many similar ones have been found at other sites of this time period (Kraft 1973:94). This would have been an enticing clue to the incredible site which lay only five feet under the ground, if it had only been identified prior to the excavation.

This site was not selected for excavation because it had yielded evidence of a Paleo-Indian occupation or that it fit the model of where Paleo-Indian sites are usually located. The initial analysis of the diagnostic and other artifacts (excluding lithic waste flakes from tool manufacturing) from the landowners' surface collections and Engelman's test pits did not indicate the presence of a Paleo-Indian occupation or even a likely artifact from that period.

Previous surface finds of fluted points in Connecticut had been on the shores of the remnants of glacial lakes, i.e. Lake Waramaug in New Preston; on high ground overlooking lakes, rivers, or likely places for game to congregate; and on the floodplains of the Housatonic and Connecticut Rivers. There was no reason to suspect a Paleo-Indian occupation on the floodplain of a river as small as the Shepaug.

This particular section of the floodplain in Washington, Connecticut was selected for excavation for two reasons. Engelman's test pits had shown an uncommonly deep, sandy alluvium with *in situ* artifacts. Although the diagnostic artifacts were not found deep in the soil profile, the occurrence of even waste flakes at greater depths indicates a human presence. The diversity of artifacts found in the field

10

where they had been plowed out of context revealed a long time period of occupation. If the same type of evidence from the rest of the field could be found in the proper stratigraphic context, we would be better able to study the culture history of the Shepaug Valley and the lifeways of each individual group.

The stratigraphic separation of artifacts according to the groups that left them is not seen frequently. This requires the gradual deposition of fine-grained soil by flooding to carefully cover the debris from a single occupation without washing it away or disturbing the relationships among the artifacts. If there is additional flooding and silting before subsequent occupants arrive to camp in the same area, the strata being accumulated will neatly separate one group's debris from that of the previous and the subsequent occupants. The opportunity was definitely present for a deeply stratified site having many separate occupations: a fine sandy soil with many bands of differing soil color and texture, as well as a wide diversity of artifacts. If only a section of the field could be found with a maximum amount of deposition, repeated occupations, and minimal disturbance by plowing and natural forces, we would have an important site.

Despite the exciting research potential, the second reason for selecting this site was that it was appropriate for a series of field schools. The site was only a few miles from the AIAI and the dormitory where the students stayed; accessible by van; and large enough to accommodate 30 people at a time. Having made the decision to spend 12 weeks in excavating this field, the remaining problem was to select the best place to start.

The most obvious place where the deepest alluvium will be found is close to the banks of a river. This section of the floodplain will be inundated during every flood cresting the banks. As the distance from the banks increases, the likelihood for frequent and deep deposition decreases rapidly. This is because minor flooding is more frequent than major flooding.

A second factor to consider is that floodwaters are carrying a far heavier and more diverse load than normal for the river. As soon as the banks are breached, the water's velocity will decrease because the effective width of its bed is increased. The decrease in velocity causes a decrease in carrying capacity, so some of the load is dropped. If the stream is carrying mostly large rocks, these will be dropped immediately when the water breaches the bank.

If archaeological sites are desired, then a section of the floodplain has to be found downstream from where the heaviest part of the load was dropped. The optimum situation is to locate a backwater or area where the floodwaters entered so slowly that only fine silt was being carried. As the water's velocity steadily decreases, even the fine silt

11

will be deposited.

The third factor is that the floodwaters have to recede as slowly as they came or the freshly deposited material and previously deposited material will be eroded as the receding waters increase in velocity. The severity of this erosion will be magnified greatly if fine-grained materials were deposited on an unprotected surface. A surface that has a heavy mat of vegetation and roots will protect underlying soils to some degree, but exposed dirt will erode very rapidly.

As if it were not a difficult enough task to locate sites meeting these three criteria, these factors have to have occurred repeatedly through time. It would be unfortunate if 10,000 years of deposition under optimum conditions were destroyed during a single massive flood, or the cutting of a new bed by a meandering river. The massive flood did occur in 1955, but a peculiar set of circumstances precluded the destruction of the site.

The only way that the site could have been protected from the meandering Shepaug River was to have tons of rocks strewn in front of the riverbank to prevent the river from cutting into it. The one natural way was for a very steeply bedded (high gradient) stream to be carrying boulders and dropping them in the right place. This is precisely what happened. An adjacent stream had the capacity during flooding to carry massive rocks by rolling them down the existing rocky bed. As these rocks were moved into the river on the alluvial fan at the mouth of the stream, the river was moving too slowly to carry them in suspension or even push them along the bottom. The river managed to carry each one only a few feet. But this was all that was necessary. The alluvial fan got wider and wider on the downstream side of the river/stream confluence.

This had the dual effect of pushing the river to the far bank where it began to cut sideways and widen its channel and of protecting the near bank from erosion. As the fan became more pronounced, the river was actually flowing around it causing an eddy or backwater. This gradually filled with gravel, pebbles, and silt because the water's velocity was decreased. The further build-up of material added to the protection of the near bank.

Having these circumstances working gradually to protect the site from destruction was still not sufficient. There had to have been repeated small-scale, gradual flood deposition over the site to bury it deeply enough so that it would not be disturbed by plowing and subsequent natural causes.

The worst of the natural causes affecting the site occurred in 1955 during a destructive hurricane when the Shepaug River was subjected to the largest flood since its formation (Peter Patton: personal communication). This was compounded in Washington where a debris dam behind a highway bridge suddenly gave way with a wall of water destroying most of the town. In descriptions of this event local residents related stories of the incredible erosion caused. The erosive force of a wall of water on an exposed field can be imagined. But it was imagined incorrectly.

The preliminary event saving the site from total destruction was the flood deposition of tons of gravel and debris on the part of the floodplain where it begins to widen. Subsequent draining did not, because it could not, erode much due to the initial deposition.

Knowing this much about the history of the field and the process of flooding, the remaining problem was to be sure that these possible events had actually occurred to protect the site and that there were actually artifacts to protect there in the first place. One of the most disappointing aspects of archaeology is to find the perfect context exhibiting deep geologic stratigraphy, lacking cultural and natural disturbance, but which is devoid of artifacts. It would have been cruelly ironic had this field been inhabited repeatedly everywhere except where the context was the best for future archaeological interpretation. On the other hand, it was like looking for a lost ring not where it was lost, but two hundred meters down the street because the light was better there. Be that as it may, if we wanted to find the artifacts in the best possible context, we had to look where the context was the best, and not where the artifacts had already been plowed from their original context.

Everything else being equal, the best context with the deepest soil deposition and the least likelihood of subsequent disturbance would be at the confluence of the Shepaug River and a minor entering stream. Due to the fluctuations of the stream and the river during 10,000 years, their locations had changed from where they were originally.

A series of test coring through the topsoil with a small diameter, hollow tube was done parallel to the river and parallel to the stream. The series parallel to the river showed nearly 1.5m (5 feet) of sandy alluvium. The series parallel to the stream moving across the floodplain perpendicular to the river showed a sudden decrease in depth from 1.5m to .80m with an increase in large pebbles and rocks mixed with the sand as we cored further from the river.

The expected context was found exactly where the corings had begun. As one moved more than 20 meters from the river the flood-deposited soil decreased very rapidly. Moving parallel to the river the flood deposition continued to be very fine grained for at least 40 meters from the confluence. Since none of the test pits dug by Engelman had been within this band, we were faced with a good news/bad news situation. Engelman's tests had been guided

13

somewhat by the surface find spots of the landowners. They had not found much in the area having the deepest layers of fine sand (bad news). The archaeological Candides, the eternal optimists, would have been overjoyed that nothing had been found here. If they were doing surface collections after plowing and didn't find anything, that meant the plow did not remove anything from context. Anything found would be right where the original occupants had left it, since the fine-grained soil shows that nature didn't disturb it, and the dearth of surface collection material showed that the plow didn't disturb it. Now if there were only something there to begin with we would really have something. Since there is only one sure way to find out what is underground, we started planning how to conduct the excavation.

EXCAVATION PROCEDURES

Once a likely location has been selected for an excavation, the worst possible action to take is to start digging. The first action should be to carefully plan all of the excavation procedures based upon the archaeologists' goals and all of the information known about the site.

The goals of archaeology have been summarized under three headings: reconstruction of culture history, determination of past lifeways, and delineation of culture process. Almost any excavation plan will enable the archaeologist to determine the date of occupations at the site. This sequence may be based upon the physical resemblance of certain diagnostic artifacts to others already known for a particular culture, or it may be an actual stratigraphic sequence showing which groups came to this one site and when, relative to one another. This type of culture history for a single site can be amplified to the state, regional, and even national level by the addition of information from many other sites.

The determination of past lifeways is more difficult and requires good associations among various artifacts and features. To determine what a particular group did during its stay at the site, it is necessary to analyze the artifacts that were left behind by a single group and determine their functions. Ecofacts such as seeds, bones, pollen, and charcoal can give further clues to the time of year, duration of occupation, use of various tools, the surrounding environment, and the size of the population. But to use ecofacts, there must be exceedingly fine associations since the interpretations are based

14

upon all of these materials which were in use contemporaneously.

The most difficult goal is to delineate culture process. Why did the people do it this way? Why didn't they do it another way? Where did they come from and why? Why did they leave? Why did their culture change? How did their culture change? The associations at a single site and a series of related sites have to be extremely good for these kinds of questions to be answered.

Archaeologists can ask many questions in each category, but only with good associations can they hope to get accurate answers. Unfortunately we do not know the associations before digging but must rely upon a detailed excavation plan to provide them. The excavation plan applies arbitrarily sized and positioned units (provenience) to understand culturally defined units (associations) from another culture.

All of the archaeologist's units of excavation are arbitrary. He uses 1.5m squares and 5cm (2 in) levels not because he thinks the people lived in 1.5m squares or that they stacked their garbage in 5cm levels, but because this is a convenient recording unit. Since he cannot guess what size units they did have, he picks one convenient to himself. The same is true of levels. For ease of recording squares are dug in vertical levels of convenient depth. If only the people had laid down a piece of aluminum foil before discarding their artifacts, the archaeologist's task would be so much easier. Since they didn't and couldn't (no Hershey Kisses to unwrap to piece the foil together), a convenient unit has to be selected. The levels used here were 5cm deep as measured with a transit and stadia rod for accuracy.

Everyone has his favorite size excavation units and his reasons for choosing them. In this case 1.5m is large enough to dig to a depth of 1.5m with comfort. There is a danger in digging deeper than the length of one side of the square not only because of cave-ins, but also the mobility problem and only having light at high noon. Larger units are difficult for beginners to keep level. The mapping frame (Plate 2) could be made conveniently to this size as was the paper for mapping the surface of each level to scale.

The 5cm vertical levels were small enough to work accurately by careful troweling or shoveling. If an artifact were missed *in situ* and found in the sifter, its precise depth could be expressed within a range only 5cm thick. The 5cm level units produced up to 30 arbitrary levels for each square, which served to separate a series of occupations which were not already separated by differences in associated artifacts or in the color or texture of soil.

The size of the excavation units were determined after a careful consideration of the entire situation: expected depth of the site judged by the depth of test corings, expected efficiency and level of expertise of the excavators, and ease of recording. It always comes back to the fact that excavation units are sized according to the goals of the excavation. We could have, as some have, recorded every single flake, artifact, and rock precisely in place. Then knowing absolutely precisely where everything was found, maps could have been made to determine the associations of everything as it was excavated. As it is now we know the exact location of some artifacts, but the remainder were mapped only to the 1.5m square and the 5cm level from which they came. Had smaller units been used the precision of the data would have been increased, but much less would have been excavated due to the increased mapping time.

There must always be trade-offs in excavation plans, but they should not be changed once the excavation has commenced. Changes in the excavation plan will not only alter the nature of the possible interpretations, but may also preclude the ability to compare data excavated previously at the same site.

The archaeologist continues to employ these excavation units he has arbitrarily selected until he discovers a cultural unit or feature such as a pit, hearth, burial, or other evidence of man's purposeful alteration of the landscape. The arbitrary units are used to record these features, but each feature is excavated as a unit separate from the surrounding soil and from other features.

Having made these decisions in advance, a grid was laid out along a 75m long north-south baseline parallel to the river. Using a transit to sight along this line, the crew drove eight-inch gutter spikes into the ground at 10m intervals. The first 10m interval was then spiked at 1.5m intervals. An east-west baseline perpendicular to the north-south line extended 4.5m. The resulting grid was subsequently expanded grid west and grid north. Fig. 2 shows the relationship of the grid to the stream and river, of the Paleo-Indian component to the non-Paleo-Indian sections (not discussed here), the numbering system used for the squares, and the relative elevations of the ground's surface. Plate 1 shows the excavation in progress.

Since the grid orientation had been determined on the basis of the depth of the fine, sandy sediments in different areas, the major dilemma well-known to all archaeologists arose: where to put the backdirt. This is not a problem to be taken lightly. We knew that twenty 1.5m squares dug to the depth of 1.5m would yield $67.5m^3$ (2000 ft^3 or 80 yd^3) or more than 50 tons of sand to move from the wrong place to the right place. We decided to put it between the long edge of the grid and the river to permit unlimited movement north-south and onto the floodplain away from the river. This proved to have been the second best location since the Paleo-Indian component was found grid north and west of where we started, but it also went to the east...under the backdirt. The best place would have been grid south, but this is obvious only with 20/20 hindsight.

The excavation began with the removal of all of the topsoil as a single unit within each square. Since its contents had been disturbed from their original contexts by plowing, 5cm levels were not used. Although there was no hope for precise associations in topsoil, the artifacts recovered during shoveling and from the 1/4 inch mesh sifter would merely define the groups which had once occupied the site (culture history) without a detailed cultural lifeways determination of each separate group being possible. Once the color change to the brown-orange subsoil was noticed, careful shoveling or troweling by 5cm levels commenced.

Although everyone began by learning the proper troweling techniques to acquaint themselves with what they were looking for and how thick 5cm was, a few graduated to a shovel. Used very carefully a shovel can skim off a thin layer of dirt so precisely that the trained user can see and hear individual stone chips and artifacts and stop the forward motion of the shovel before they have been dislodged very far from their original context. Since we required accuracy first to know as precisely as possible where everything came from, a few human "woodchucks" were discouraged from trying the shovel techniques. Shoveling was not used when we were definitely into the Paleo-Indian component.

The usual technique was to trowel the dirt in thin layers. The dirt was placed into pails and taken to the sifter. The artifacts, if any, were then placed into the envelope or bag kept with the person in that square. Each bag was labeled with the site number, square number, level, date, and excavator's name. This redundancy precluded problems in the laboratory trying to determine who was responsible for an incorrect label and what the label should have been.

When an artifact was found *in situ,* the mapping frame was placed on the gutter spikes at the corners of the square. Since the gutter spikes remained in place until the square was completed, every level's map was precisely superimposed over that of every other level. This also ensured an accurate alignment with adjacent squares since every square shared two nails with each adjacent one. Since the gutter spikes were driven into the pillars (Plate 1), they were maintained as much as possible until the very end. When they were taken down, the positions of their nails were noted so that the cobble layer could be mapped with respect to all of the upper levels (Plate 2).

Although no definite features were found in the Paleo-Indian component, flotation of living floors was an extremely important part of the excavation plan. The flotation process is the recovery of small-scale plant and animal remains using water seperation. Buckets of dirt from the occupation level were taken to a washtub in the river. The tub's bottom had been replaced with window-screen mesh and the tub was immersed in water almost to its rim. The dirt was dumped into the tub and agitated. Most of the very fine sand washed through the mesh.

A tea strainer was used to scoop off the floating material (light fraction) and place it on film pans to dry. The heavy fraction consisting of gravel and water-saturated charcoal was also dumped from the mesh onto the drying pans. All of this was later examined to separate tiny artifacts, charcoal, and possible seeds.

When the component had been totally excavated, the walls were profiled (Plate 3). The first step in the profiling was to carefully trowel the wall to remove loose dirt and to achieve a vertical surface. The wall was then sprayed with water to highlight the sometimes subtle differences in soil color and texture in each discrete band. While the wall was still wet, the person mapping carefully cut fine lines into the wall to delineate the boundaries of each band. The vertical profiler made from a hollow metal tube with holes drilled at 10cm intervals had a series of weighted string lines to facilitate making a scale drawing of the soil bands.

Figs. 3, 4, 5, 6 show the finished vertical profiles of the walls surrounding the Paleo-Indian component. Because the same sequence of soil levels recur, they were very useful during the excavation. Since the Paleo-Indian component was always found in the clay-coated sand band immediately beneath the white sand with gravel and immediately above the cobbles, it was easy to see which squares would be most likely to be productive and which would not be. A complete description of physical setting and subsurface geology follows in the next section.

The excavation plan used at 6LF21 was not devised specifically for a Paleo-Indian site. It served its purpose well, but would definitely have to be altered if we were to return to the same site knowing what we know now. The reason for the change is that new interpretations require a new excavation technique specifically designed to collect certain types of data. If the same techniques were used, the data would be collected according to the same arbitrary units. A change in these units would cause a change in the archaeologist's idea of their meaning for the data at hand.

PHYSICAL SETTING

The site is located on the first terrace of the floodplain of the Shepaug River in Washington, Connecticut. The surface of the site was 3.4m (11.5 ft) above the river at the time of excavation. Although the soil matrix is classified as Windsor loamy fine sand (Gonick, Shearin, and Hill 1970: Map 84), the flood of 1955 deposited a light to medium gravel on the surface. While much of the gravel was bulldozed into piles and trucked away to repair flood damage, the remaining stone is slowly settling into the topsoil.

Because of the past farming activities, the ground cover in the field is limited to grass and equisetum. The field is bordered by native deciduous trees and a few planted evergreens. The paucity of native plants in the immediate vicinity of the site is due to the farming and is decidedly atypical of the Shepaug Valley in general.

The prehistoric setting of the site is the archaeologist's and geologist's reconstruction of what the site looked like when the people first arrived to establish a camp. A careful study of the appearance of the site, including some of the reasons why it was attractive to the inhabitants, will provide clues to finding similar sites of comparable dates.

Prior to the first occupation of the site the cobble layer (Plate 4, Fig. 7) was deposited. The geologist who studied this, Dr. Peter Patton of Wesleyan University, came to the conclusion that it was a debris fan resulting from a single massive flooding episode (1978). Since the cobbles are highly similar to the ones in the stream bed currently adjacent to the site, he believes that the stream was diverted from its current banks for a very short period of time causing the deposition of the rocks on the site.

We were at first very dubious that such a narrow stream could have transported such massive rocks until we examined the rocks currently in the stream bed. The largest rocks in the stream are no larger than the ones at the site. The stream did not actually carry the rocks in suspension but moved them along its bed. The force of the water and the very steep gradient was more than sufficient to transport them.

The sudden termination of the cobble layer at the extreme eastern edge of the excavation can be explained in two ways. Either the debris fan entered the river at this point or the gradient suddenly decreased some distance from the river. Although more geological studies are being conducted in the entire Shepaug River Valley to better understand flooding episodes and the previous courses of the river, the clues from the excavation at this site suggest the former. Immediately grid east of the debris fan is a coarse sand which grades to a fine sand grid north and south at levels far deeper than the base of the cobbles. The elevation of the cobble layer at this point is 1.9m above the river and less than 15m from the edge of the channel. This is an even steeper gradient than in the excavated portion of the site having the cobbles. Since there are no obvious obstructions which would have prevented cobbles from continuing downslope and the fine sand of the adjacent areas indicates deposition during a period of slow-moving water typical of the river and not a flooding stream, the inescapable conclusion is that the debris fan terminated in the river and not some distance from its banks. The power of the water transporting such large rocks would have been more than sufficient to have eroded the fine sand between the cobbles and the river had a barrier of this nature been present. The fine sand must have been deposited subsequent to the cobbles.

If these were the agents responsible for the deposition of cobbles and the fine sand surrounding them, then the physical setting was a stream and river confluence having a large cleared area covered by cobbles. Judging from its homogeneity the fine clay-coated sand forming the primary matrix for all of the Paleo-Indian artifacts was deposited by a single flooding episode of the river prior to the arrival of the inhabitants. The reason for the distribution of the artifacts throughout the zone has been mentioned previously and will be discussed in detail below.

Now the people have to be attracted to this physical setting. Although the broad floodplain was a logical path for travel along the river, the actual river banks were not. In most areas covered by soil, trees would have been growing to the water's edge. Debris from trees falling into the river in addition to flood debris would impede travel. However, the best camping area would be as close to the water as possible, assuming a cleared area could be found. The fine sand covering the cobbles would make such an area: open, well-drained, and close to drinking water.

An extra added attraction here would be the actual confluence of the river and stream. Within a few hundred meters of the site today is a river; stream; backwater areas slowly filling with silt to become still, shallow pools, swamps, bogs, and eventually dry land; open floodplain; and low hills with sunny and shaded flanks. A similar variety of econiches 10,000 years ago would have supported a very diverse plant and animal population. In addition the identification of red oak and either juniper or white cedar charcoal from the Paleo-Indian occupation area adds diversity and even a better reason to camp in this one locale: the carrying capacity (ability to support life) of a deciduous hardwood forest is much higher than an evergreen forest dominated by pine or spruce.

20

CHAPTER TWO

The analysis of any archaeological site or collection is a series of objective observations to accurately identify and describe all of the data. Data include artifacts, ecofacts (charcoal), maps, drawings, measurements, and other observations made during the excavation and analysis. While a simple identification may be only the name of an individual artifact, a complete description would include raw material, manufacturing techniques, size, weight, and evidence of utilization. Once the items have been identified and described individually, associations among artifacts are discussed. From these associations the intensive analysis develops into a meaningful interpretation.

Analysis is not an end, but a means to an end. All observations have been designed to determine the regularities inherent in the artifacts and ecofacts, which will permit an interpretation of the culture of the people who once occupied the site. The range of consistencies in human behavior is extremely broad. Some of the patterns noted are typical of all people everywhere who have ever lived; of only North America peoples; of only Paleo-Indian; of only Eastern Paleo-Indian; of only Northeastern Paleo-Indian; and possibly only of Connecticut Paleo-Indians; and of only the single group who occupied this site.

The recognition and explanation of inconsistencies must also come from the analysis. The complete analysis will be a record of everything that reinforces the interpretation, as well as the data that do not fit. The presentation of this material is fuel for future research.

To make the data presented as useful as possible it is necessary to understand the excavation techniques as well as the analytical ones. A large number of the apparent associations was a result of the arbitrary excavation units of squares and levels. Had different sized units been placed in a different configuration the associations would have been different. Just because the associations were different, however, does not imply that the interpretations would differ. The researcher who thinks the arbitrary units of the excavator have distorted the interpretation must devise a different excavation plan for a future excavation. It is impossible to replace and re-dig the data.

The researcher who accepts the excavation procedures, but wishes to re-analyze the actual artifacts and ecofacts using different observations has a much easier task. This study can be done very easily since all of the artifacts and research notes are stored at the American Indian Archaeological Institute in Washington, Connecticut. While it seems only reasonable that all of the data from a single site should be stored in one location, this is more the exception than the rule. Since most Paleo-Indian sites were either on the surface, disturbed, or known for a long time, they have been visited repeatedly by collectors and different excavators. Each group stored its data separately making an analysis or re-analysis difficult.

Before the actual analysis began, all of the artifacts were washed, sorted and cataloged. Because this procedure was completed within a month of the close of the excavation while everything was still fresh in everyone's mind, it was easy to recognize and correct obviously incorrectly labeled artifacts.

Cataloging included a drawing of every specimen (excluding waste flakes), all provenience information, type of raw material, description of characteristics not obvious in the drawing, and a unique catalog number. Each individual specimen got a separate card, except waste flakes which were grouped onto a single card for each different level within each square.

The catalog number, 77-2-1/31.1.12, appearing on a specimen meant that it was the 12th specimen cataloged from the 1st level of the 31st excavation unit at the 1st site (6LF21) excavated by AIAI in 1977. The levels were numbered sequentially from the topsoil through each of the 5cm arbitrary levels. Precise depths were assigned numbers as were indeterminate depths resulting from wall cave-ins.

This system has many advantages. All of the cards for all artifacts from a single level are sequential as are all levels from a single square and all squares at a single site. The artifacts are stored in precisely the same way. One cabinet has all of the boxes containing specimens in sequential order labeled by catalog number and original provenience. Within each box are the original envelopes arranged in sequential order by levels. With the exception of those containing waste flakes, most envelopes contain only a single artifact.

While the cataloging was time-consuming, it was necessary to prevent accidental admixture of data from different squares or levels. If an unlabeled specimen was found on the table after analysis or was returned to the wrong envelope, there would be no way to determine where it belonged. Individual catalog cards permit data recording where it will do the most good: right with a drawing of the specimen. The cards are so much easier to look through to become familiar with a collection than are hundreds of individual envelopes.

The first step in the analysis was to separate all of the retouched and utilized artifacts from the waste flakes. While this had been done prior to cataloging, additional specimens were identified. Several additional specimens were even found on the third and fourth sortings. This does not reflect upon the sorters' inattention, but upon their lack of experience with Paleo-Indian materials and the very subtle nature of the edge wear. Subsequent finds in the collection also reflect the amazing consistency among the discrete artifact types. Once these consistencies were noted on the specimens found first, subsequent identifications were facilitated.

Before the associations of chippage and artifacts could be analyzed, it was necessary to re-define the arbitrary 5cm excavation levels in terms of the actual geologic stratigraphy at the site. Since the deepest level of the site sloped very steeply towards the river (Fig. 3) and all of the measurements had been made with respect to vertical lines, the same cultural strata occurred at different depths in different squares. Since the last 5cm level on top of the cobble layer at the bottom of the site was the deepest level at which any cultural evidence could be found, this was considered the first level of the Paleo-Indian occupation. Subsequent 5cm levels moving vertically were assigned sequential numbers up to 13. Thus, regardless of the depth below the ground's surface, the deepest evidence of Paleo-Indian was in the sand immediately above the cobble layer and assigned the level number 1. Because the top of the Paleo-Indian occupation zone could be seen in the wall profiles and in the sudden decrease in flint chips recovered, it was obvious where to stop the numbering.

All of the debitage was sorted into flint and quartz chips. All of each type of chippage from a single level within a square was counted and weighed on a triple beam balance calibrated in tenths of grams. Tables 1, 2, 3, 4 summarize the counts and weights of flint and quartz chips within each level, each square, and the entire site. Figs. 8, 9 show the distribution of chippage throughout the Paleo-Indian component.

Other tools used in the analysis were dial calipers calibrated in tenths of millimeters, a mechanical protractor calibrated in degrees, polar coordinate graph paper calibrated in degrees, a 10X hand lens, and a binocular microscope with 40X and 100X magnification. The extra cost of dial calipers is worth it for the added accuracy and decrease in eye fatigue when thousands of measurements must be made.

The analysis of the distribution and associations of the bifacial thinning flakes and other artifacts (Fig. 10) was far more complex and time-consuming. Since these are discussed in detail in a separate section, only the general procedure will be mentioned now.

The most difficult problem was determining the pertinent observations. Appendix A outlines the observations made on all specimens. Other observations were not recorded since they are obvious from the Plates but are important traits to consider in comparing collections from different sites. Still other observations were highly significant and consistent in this analysis. Observations should not be made merely for the sake of making them. If they cannot be shown to have usefulness in describing an artifact's appearance, function, etc., it is a waste of time to record them.

Edge wear analysis conducted on the specimens began by scanning them with a 10X hand lens. Using a 40X binocular microscope the entire perimeter was scanned. The laterals were again scanned using a 100X magnification. The medial section of each specimen was scanned with a 10X and 40X magnification for evidence of wear due to hafting.

Equally important as the discovery of flake scars and striations is the determination of their meaning. Edge wear is a cumulative process. All of the functions served by a particular tool may be evidenced if the duration of use was sufficiently long or intensive. Traumatic edge wear such as impact fractures may or may not occur even on an intensively utilized specimen.

The absence of edge wear does not mean a tool was discarded prior to use, nor does the presence of edge wear indicate a long-term use. Errett Callahan's well-publicized butchering of Ginsberg the elephant (Park 1978) and Robert Funk's experiments with flint knives and scrapers (1976:215) show that although the degree of edge wear increases with the duration of a tool's use, some materials (hide and wood) can be worked for long periods of time without discernible microscopic edge wear; while bone working can cause extensive wear almost immediately. The absence of edge wear does not mean that the tool's edge was not rejuvenated for use in the same function or for different functions.

The range of possible functions for utilized flakes and all artifacts exhibiting edge wear must be considered carefully in light of recent use-wear studies conducted by John Brink (1978) and others. Use-wear studies were best brought to the attention of archaeologists through the work of S.A. Semenov (1964). Since that time, the lure of confidently assigned precise functions to every utilized edge has prompted an ever-increasing amount of work. While the confidence is still there, the number of variables affecting edge wear has increased as dramatically as the research.

The raw material category has to be re-defined to include every single lithic source and not just flint, jasper, and quartz. Each has different properties affecting its durability, susceptibility to flaking, etc. Wood has to be studied as not only hardwoods and softwoods, but also as separate species and states of seasoning. For every study completed and use-wear documented critics will cite a new list of variables to be considered in the next study. When all of the variables can be identified and the resultant edge wear documented, then a final decision can be made as to what caused a particular pattern.

Brink's (1978) experimental study on endscrapers identified four types of edge damage: microflaking, rounding, polish, and striations. Microflaking is the removal of tiny flakes caused by the application of steady pressure or force along the edge of the ventral side, resulting in three types of scars, *step, hinge,* and *feather,* which can occur as part of the manufacturing process or during utilization. Step scars end at an abrupt right angle. Hinge scars have the right angle step and a tiny lip of stone overhanging the step. Feather scars lack the abrupt termination and appear as shallow, roughly circular concavities intersecting the edge. These scars can be crushed or nibbled. Crushing occurs as poorly defined, but intensive scarring, while nibbling scars are parallel to one another and arranged in an orderly fashion perpendicular to the edge (Brink 1978: 50-55).

Rounding occurs as either the breaking off of tiny flakes or the abrasion of material from the edge. The effect is to leave an edge smoother than one which had been only flaked. This is different from polishing which occurs parallel to the edge on either the ventral or dorsal face. They are similar in that they are abrasive processes but differ in the location of the abrasion and the resulting smoothness. Polished edges will have a sheen or luster in marked contrast to the immediately adjacent dorsal or ventral faces.

Striations are scratches that occur on either the dorsal or ventral faces extending varying distances from and at different angles to the working edge. In Brink's study only the inclusion of silt on the surfaces being scraped produced striations. They were not observed under any other conditions.

The most important conclusion he draws relevant to the current analysis is "...with the exception of bone working, microflake utilization scars did not differ in form or distribution from manufacturing scars. Two of the experimental tasks (hide de-hairing and fleshing) failed to produce any microflaking, while two other tasks (antler and dry hide scraping) produced only minimal amounts of microflaking" (1978:116).

Rounding and polishing occurred in wood, bone, antler, and hide working to varying degrees. Since these did not occur during manufacturing or on non-utilized specimens, they are seen as excellent indicators of use. The nature and intensity of wear varied with different materials, making them also a good indicator of what was being worked.

I am strongly suspicious that the flint is the prime variable in determining whether certain types of edge wear will be present or noticeable if they were present. The flint at 6LF21 has a very grainy appearance with banding or other inclusions. It is not as lustrous as a Brandon flint or other Old World specimens studied by Semenov (1964). I would never suggest that edge wear studies be abandoned until a perfect type of lithic material is at hand, but at this site the lithic material used revealed its edge damage/wear quite well at 10X, with 40X useful in a tiny minority of the specimens. The more subtle form of edge wear - striations - was not seen on any specimen at any magnification, due to the nature of the lithic material. The functions suggested by the artifacts themselves should have produced striations, but none was seen.

The next task is to examine the recorded data for the best manner of presentation. All of the data will not apply to all of the artifacts. Separate tables for bifacial thinning flakes, channel flakes, etc. will facilitate further interpretation. The Tables contain observations which were not used in the current interpretation, but which will be of comparative value for future analysis by other researchers.

Because Brink's conclusions on the presence of microflaking on unused tools were based solely upon the sample of thirty endscrapers which were made by Cort Sims of the University of Alberta, there is no way to differentiate unintentional manufacturing microflaking from utilization microflaking in a prehistoric sample. Or is there? After a close examination of more than 7300 waste flakes from 6LF21 only 16 were identified as evidencing nibbling, nicks, and/or polish. While it may be only a coincidence, it seems highly fortuitous that only .2% of all of the waste flakes would exhibit closely spaced, parallel nibbling scars. Not only would the knapper have had to produce this type of microflaking unintentionally only .2% of the time, but also on the laterals instead of the ends. The most serendipitous occurrence of all was that the nibbling sometimes occurred not only in more than one place on the same flake, but that all of this occurred during the detachment of the flake from the core or from a single flake previously detached on the dorsal face.

Given the unlikelihood that concentrated nibbling on waste flakes can be a result of manufacturing, Brink's observations should be qualified. When tools are made by the removal of many flakes to create a working edge, the likelihood is very great that individual flake scars will occur which resemble those of microflaking due to utilization. Utilization will be evidenced by the regularity of these microflakes not only in their location, but also in their variety: step, hinge, or feather. Exceptions to this will occur with the type of stone being used, the material being worked, the intensity of use, and multiple tasks, among others.

Because feather scars and nibbling are the most frequently evidenced form of microflaking in this collection, their occurrence in Brink's scraping study will be considered in detail along with polishing. When scraping wood, microflaking occurred whenever a projection (knot) was struck. Because softer woods yield to the scraper and are finer grained than hardwoods, nibbling is more likely than step or hinge fractures. Scraping of hardwoods created severe step and hinge fractures.

Bone scraping created step and hinge fractures more frequently than feather scars but was the only work which left ventral scars. This is highly significant since many of the utilized flakes had ventral scars which were nibbled. Using the microflaking trends from soft and hard woods, future bone scraping experiments should be done to try to replicate nibbling by varying the types of bone being scraped, degree of pressure, contact angle, and material preparation.

Ventral wear in bone working assumes that the dorsal face is up. Were the dorsal face down in working bone, the wear would be dorsal; in working any other material the wear would be ventral. The modern replicator cannot be guided too much by the motor habits he thinks were employed but should try to work from the wear patterns back to the motor habits. This tack has been taken very successfully with historic replicative work at Old Sturbridge Village, Massachusetts, and should be applied to prehistoric cases as well (John Worrell, personal communication).

Rounding and polishing occurred together on wood and antler scraping, but erratically on hide scraping. Bone scraping produced a wider band of polish than scraping antler, and softer woods produced more than hardwoods. These results are consistent with the microflaking: the softer materials produced the least severe edge wear. Hides are very soft and produced almost no wear. Nibbling, rounding, and polish could be found in soft wood working and possibly in careful bone working. Once antler and hardwoods are being scraped, nibbling is replaced by step and hinge fractures and the degree of polish and rounding is decreased or takes longer to develop. Another conclusion is that the presence of only rounding and/or polishing could be accounted for solely by hide working. Microflaking would have been evidenced after a few hundred strokes on any other material.

This discussion has included scraping functions and not cutting. Semenov's description (1964:101-104) of Upper Paleolithic meat knives which included the cutting of strips of meat, as well as separating meat from hides in the skinning process, includes prominent dorsal and ventral polish. Although he had no way of determining the duration of their use, he suggests that they were used for long periods to achieve fully polished edges. Callahan's recent use of flint knives in butchering Ginsburg the elephant (Park 1978) showed no wear at the end. Because meat is so soft, the duration of cutting it prior to edge wear would have been extremely long if one can use Callahan's and Brink's observations on how long it takes for edge wear when working very soft materials.

Although meat cutting functions could have been served by the utilized flakes exhibiting polish, the localized occurrence of polish on a segment of a single lateral could only have been a result of cutting thin strips at a steep angle repeatedly in the same place on the flake. Given the duration factor, meat cutting wear on waste flakes should be discounted in favor of cutting other materials. The range of possible materials which could be cut and produce the edge wear evidenced in Table 9 is limited to the very soft ones, i.e. hides, plant fibers, and flesh. Cutting functions can be expanded to a few fine-grained materials which will yield to an acute edge slitting them or wedging them apart, i.e. reeds, dried bones, small saplings.

The edge wear on the utilized flakes includes nibbling, which can only occur with soft materials; polish which requires very fine-grained materials to rub over the surface parallel to the working edge for long periods of time; and nicks caused by impacting resistant spots. Extensive replicative work will be necessary on raw materials known to have been available to the Paleo-Indian peoples of Western Connecticut to determine the most likely tasks served by these utilized flakes.

SOURCE OF LITHIC MATERIALS

Both of the different lithic materials, flint and quartz, worked for tools could have been found within three miles of the site. Cortical flakes from water-polished flint cobbles could have come from the

28

Shepaug River. During the excavation, the crew took a short walk along the banks of the river adjacent to the site and found several small flint cobbles. While these cobbles were significantly smaller than ones from which the cortical flakes found in the excavation would have come, the source seems obvious. Since the banks were extensively altered by erosion and the deposition of debris during the 1955 hurricane, the currently exposed gravel has either covered or replaced that present 10,000 years ago. However, the current presence of flint cobbles does suggest an upstream source which could have been responsible for the appearance of cobbles at intervals in the past. Despite repeated attempts to find an upstream outcropping which could have been eroded by the river or a glacial deposit from which the flint cobbles could have been derived by the river in flood, we did not find one. We did, however, find a very likely source not far from the Shepaug River's confluence with Bee Brook north of the town of Washington.

During a survey prior to the proposed construction of new homes, a multi-component site was located on a series of knolls overlooking what is currently a swamp drained by an intermittent stream. Although no diagnostic Paleo-Indian artifacts were found, the retouching on some specimens was highly familiar. The most important artifact from the survey was a chunk of flint having naturally squared corners and a flat dorsal face. This type of chunk could only have been caused by the intrusion of the molten flint into an existing bedrock such as limestone. This was not cobble flint but quarry flint.

Since there are no known flint outcroppings in the state of Connecticut and massive outcroppings occur in the Hudson Valley, the easy explanation for any flint was that it was brought in from the west. Since flint does not have legs, there are only three possible explanations for its occurrence at sites in Connecticut: (1) trade, (2) stocking up, and (3) fetching. A regular trade in flint from groups living close to the source through a series of middlemen to those living in Connecticut is dubious. If these groups were as small, mobile, and dispersed as the archaeological record indicates, trade would have been a very haphazard way of distributing an essential commodity. Trade also indicates a surplus of at least two items. Flint was obviously a surplus commodity for the people living on tons of it, but what would they want to obtain in trade that they could not get for themselves?

The second alternative is that the people traveling into Connecticut knew that it was flint-free and stocked up on their way through the Hudson Valley. This would have been a straight line distance of 100 km (60 miles), but closer to 160 km (100 miles) taking the easy way through passes and up river valleys. I would favor this if it weren't for the cortical flakes. Carrying dead weight does not make sense. Quarries are littered with decortication and trimming flakes from people who removed as much of the unusable portion of the stone as possible before leaving. The second objection is the absence of direct evidence they were ever in the Hudson Valley or even had a need to travel that far to fulfill basic needs.

The third alternative is to send someone back to the Hudson Valley where you saw a great supply of flint but forgot to get enough to last until the next trip. I think that life was hard enough without somebody making it harder. If they had depleted their flint supply, another locally available stone, quartz, would have had similar traits of durability and sharpness. Since these were not permanent camps occupied by large numbers, it would have made more sense to move the entire camp closer to the supply than to send one person on a couple of hundred miles round trip.

In summary I find it impossible to believe that the flint tools found at this site were manufactured here from chunks quarried in the Hudson Valley. This does not rule out the possibility that some finished flint tools were made from Hudson Valley flint and brought to the site, used, and discarded. However, the chunks being worked here were more likely derived from local or nearly local sources.

The cobble flint could be explained by water-polished pieces currently found in the Shepaug River, but where could quarry chunks lacking a water-polished surface have come from if not from the only known sources in the Hudson Valley? The answer is: from currently unknown sources in Connecticut which are similar to those in far eastern New York and southern Massachusetts.

Shortly after the news of the importance of this site was made public, Dr. Eau Zen of the United States Geological Survey informed me that the Stockbridge limestone formation (Unit C) has bands of chert (flint) up to 30cm thick in outcroppings near Millerton, New York, on the far northwestern border of Connecticut and continuing north to East Hillsdale, New York (September 1, 1977 personal correspondence). While these outcroppings seem rather far from the Shepaug River, their accessibility is enhanced by the nature of the Housatonic Valley, which leads directly towards them.

However, there is really no need to hypothesize a trip up the Housatonic, since the Stockbridge limestone formation is found in Connecticut. The town of Marbledale is not only just a few miles from the Paleo-Indian site, but the flint chunk found in the survey mentioned above was found only a few hundred yards from a Stockbridge outcrop.

Despite a non-intensive, fruitless search for remnants of flint bands in existing outcroppings in the immediate vicinity, all is not lost. The obvious local outcroppings of Stockbridge limestone were metamorphosed to marble which was used extensively by the early occupants of Marbledale. Although no mention has been found of flint bands within the marble, (hypothetically) there were once local outcroppings of Stockbridge marble containing bands of flint. Paleo-Indian quarried the flint available close to the surface, and subsequent occupants of Marbledale removed the traces of quarrying, as well as flint bands. While this theory logically explains all of the available evidence, it will not be proved until undisturbed Stockbridge marble strata containing flint can be found.

The source of the only other utilized stone at the site, quartz, is easy to identify. Quartz cobbles are found in and along the river and in thick bands in Hidden Valley, located north of Washington along the Shepaug River.

DATING AND IDENTIFICATION OF CHARCOAL

A wood charcoal sample submitted to the United States Geological Survey Radiocarbon Laboratory was dated to 10,190 +/− 300 years B.P.: 8240 B.C. (W-3931). The significance of the date can be better understood after a discussion of terminology, associations, and comparisons to other Paleo-Indian components in the Northeast.

Since B.P. stands for Before Present, why is the B.C. date only 8240? By convention *present* was defined as 1950 because this is when carbon-14 dating came into general use; a standard is needed so that the "present" does not change every year; and it is easier to subtract using a number ending in 50 rather than 49 or 52. (I think that 2000 should have been accepted to make it easier still. Since the number is arbitrary, why not make it easy as well?)

To prevent mixing multiple samples from the same site or same researcher, each radiocarbon laboratory has a code and assigns a number to each sample. Sample W-3931's date will not be confused with any other Paleo-Indian dates if it is always expressed with the laboratory code letter and number.

The date of 10,190 is not a precise measurement. Because the carbon-14 dating process is not capable of accurately measuring the age of a charcoal sample to the nearest 10 years, the date must be expressed with an error factor, in this case 300 years. This means that the actual date of the sample is actually between 10,490 and 9890 years B.P. Since the error factor is determined statistically, it will vary from sample to sample and usually increases as older charcoal is dated. Even with the error factor of 300 years, there is only 66.7% likelihood that the actual date is within the range given. The error factor could have been reduced by the averaging of many dated samples from the same context.

The error factor is always present because no sample is so pure that there is a 100% chance that some form of contamination is not affecting the outcome. Since carbon is found in all living things, the atmosphere, and many minerals which dissolve in water, it is no wonder that contamination occurs. Contamination commenced when the wood was burned making the charcoal that was dated. Contaminating factors continued until it was dated.

When the sample was taken from the ground, it was not touched by human hands (skin, moisture) but only with clean metal tools. It was dried and sorted to remove obvious contaminants (ants, root hairs). Further processing in the laboratory prior to dating removed material dissolved in ground water which might have come out of solution and settled into the charcoal. Since every possible contaminant cannot be removed, the date is not perfect.

The 10,190 years are not the number of calendar years which have elapsed, but are radiocarbon years. Since the radioactive decay of carbon-14 to carbon-13 and stable carbon-12 progresses at a relatively constant rate, one would expect that one radiocarbon year would equal any other one. If this were the case, then a simple conversion formula could be devised to yield calendar years. It is not the case because the ratio of carbon-14 to carbon-12, which is present in the atmosphere to be absorbed by all living things, is not constant.

The amount of carbon and its compounds in the atmosphere is affected by solar radiation, sunspots, burning of fossil fuels, and differences in forest cover on land masses. Since all of these activities affect the entire world at the same time, radiocarbon dating gives the same results on contemporaneous samples from everywhere. All sites dated to 10,000 radiocarbon years ago actually were occupied at the same time, but the date of the occupation was not 10,000 calendar years ago.

Correction factors for radiocarbon dates have been worked out using tree-ring dating, which is much closer to giving an actual date in calendar years and does not have the large fluctuations in carbon to cause problems. This problem is discussed in detail by Elizabeth Ralph, H.N. Michael, and M.C. Han (1974:1-20), Don Dragoo (1974:21-29), and Bruce Rippeteau (1974:29-37).

The charcoal which was dated came from a small, stained area within the clay-coated sand zone of the Paleo-Indian component. When this zone in square 9.0N4.5W was being troweled, a stain about 10cm in diameter suddenly appeared. The stain did not originate at a higher level and intrude into the Paleo-Indian component, but was sealed within it. Since this stain was within the size range of postmolds, a vertical cut was made to examine the cross section. A second vertical cut perpendicular to the first was also made. The cross section was a solid mass of charcoal flecks and chunks with an erratic outline.

Although postmolds are usually quite symmetrical, like the original posts, this is not necessarily the case when a charred post is found. Postmolds made by the rotting of the original post or its removal and subsequent filling of the hole by darker-colored soil would not endure for 10,000 years without extraordinary circumstances. All of the organic material would have been totally decayed, the dark color would have leached out, and all trace of previous structures would have been lost. This is not the case with postmolds resulting from a structure burning. As the fire consumes the above-ground structure, the parts of the posts in the ground will dry rapidly. As the fire burns closer to the ground, the likelihood of charring increases because of the decrease in oxygen necessary for complete combustion. The underground parts of the posts will not burn completely but char until the fire dies out completely. As the fire consumes the structure, the posts are subjected to stress and will lean or come completely out of the ground.

The underground charring of parts of the post or the dispersal of charcoal into the holes from the newly-collapsed structure will yield asymmetrical postmolds or charcoal-filled holes where posts once were. The charcoal for the carbon-14 sample was taken from just such an area. Although it was the size of a postmold and lacked the regularity in both of the vertical cuts, the charcoal mass was very dense and had definite, sharp, but erratic boundaries. The sharpness of the boundaries precludes interpreting this as a charred root, animal burrowing, or generalized charcoal wash due to flooding.

The charcoal sample was found within the Paleo-Indian component and was decidedly not intrusive. Although the nearest diagnostic artifacts were less than 75cm away in adjacent squares, the concentration of flint waste flakes above and below the sample location and the evidence that this is one single occupation provided the necessary associations.

The other acceptably dated Paleo-Indian sites in the Northeast are in the same time range. The Debert site [Fig. 1 (1)] in Nova Scotia (MacDonald 1968:53) yielded a series of dates which averaged 10,600 +/− 47 years B.P. Charles McNett's work at Shawnee-Minisink [Fig. 1 (8)] near the Delaware Water Gap in eastern Pennsylvania yielded two dates, 10,590 +/− 300 B.P. (W-2994) and 10,750 +/− 600 B.P. (1977). In addition to these is a questionable

33

date from excavations at Dutchess Quarry Cave [Fig. 1 (7)] in New York of 12,530 + / − 370 B.P. (Funk 1977:322). The Debert and Shawnee-Minisink dates are very close to the one from 6LF21 for similar tool kits. The wide spatial separation of the three sites and the proximity of their dates does raise some intriguing questions about the nature of Paleo-Indian movements on a seasonal, yearly, generational, and continent-wide dispersal basis.

The date from Dutchess Quarry Cave came from bone collagen instead of wood charcoal. Although the association of the collagen from caribou bones was with a single fluted point, no other Paleo-Indian artifacts were recovered. The extreme age of this date for a fluted point could be explained in two ways. The fluted point could have settled from a subsequent occupation into an older context along with "southern flying squirrel, woodrat, pine mouse, elk, passenger pigeon, and turtles" (Guilday 1969:24-25.) This type of admixture can occur in rockshelters and caves due to the burrowing of hibernating animals. Since there is no source of regular soil deposition, the same deposits are subjected to a lot more churning than would be the case on a regularly flooded area.

However, since the caribou bones had been broken intentionally, man must have been the cause. Also man and caribou could have contemporaneously occurred during post-glacial times giving validity to the association of the fluted point and the bones. Now the possibility must be raised about the accuracy of the date. Had the date been from wood charcoal, the accuracy would be more difficult to challenge or to lay to contamination. The use of bone collagen for C-14 dating can give unreliable results which may be too old or too young. The Dutchess Quarry association of man and caribou may be acceptable, but a date for Northeastern Paleo-Indian 2000 years earlier than all other indications must await further substantiation.

The usefulness of carbon-14 dating in establishing the chronological outline of man's occupation in each section of the world cannot be doubted. The laboratory fees are low, the samples can be processed quickly, they are easy to collect, and the universal occurrence of carbon in so many forms makes almost any site datable. The only problem is that all of these advantages are actually disguised disadvantages.

Nearly everyone I have ever talked to knows that charcoal can be dated. People want to date every piece of charcoal they find to determine how old the site is. The date received is the age of the charcoal, not the age of the site. The age of the site is a result of the correct association of the dated charcoal with diagnostic artifacts. If there are no artifacts, you are the proud owner of a 15,000-year-old piece of charred wood that could have been from a forest fire. If the associations are incorrect, you could have a 500-year-old fluted point and a 10,000-year-old beer can. The association is everything or the date is nothing.

Once a good association has been assured with diagnostic artifacts identical to those found in similar contexts 10 miles away, why bother to date it again? The carbon-14 date from the previous sites has served your purposes. It has provided the necessary temporal outline for diagnostic artifacts. When the diagnostic artifacts have been found in nearby areas, they can be used to date other ones. The reason they are diagnostic is that their styles have been associated with the same range of dates in the past.

Dating old things is more accurate than dating new things. An error factor of 200 years for a site about 10,000 years old is only wrong by 2%, but the same error factor for a site about 2,000 years old is off by 10%. Additionally, there are far better techniques for dating more recent sites once the basic carbon-14 chronology has been established.

Don't be lulled into the false security of a few grams of charcoal being able to "validate" a site having many components and uncertain associations. The use of carbon-14 dating to determine which associations are valid and which are not is invalid, unscientific, and worthless. Carbon-14 is not a panacea or a *deus ex machina* which will salvage disturbed contexts. Its use should be limited to regions lacking a dated chronological sequence, diagnostic artifacts not previously found in a datable context, and to situations where existing dates have an extremely broad time span or are in conflict.

Despite circumstances meeting these criteria, unexpected results often occur. During the summer of 1978, I received a call from a friend excavating a multi-component site. He had found a poorly-preserved animal skeleton with a quartz projectile point in a cervical vertebra. The medium dog-sized animal was in a dug pit with other non-diagnostic artifacts. Because the quartz point did not fit existing typologies, he wanted to have a C-14 date done. The results came back as post 1950 A.D. (GX-5890-G) with a note that the sample showed evidence of radioactive carbon from atmospheric testing of atomic weapons. You cannot be right all of the time.

At 6LF21 a far more significant use was found for charcoal samples collected from 7.5N1.5W at .70-.75m and 9.0N3.0W at .90-.95m below datum. These were submitted to Dr. Bruce Hoadley, Wood Science and Technology, University of Massachusetts, Amherst. The first sample was red oak and either juniper or white cedar. The second sample was identified as either juniper or white cedar. The significance of these identifications follows.

ENVIRONMENTAL RECONSTRUCTIONS

To better understand any culture it is necessary to study their material remains (artifacts) in a larger context. A significant aspect of the larger context is the natural environment. With an understanding of the opportunities presented to and the limitations imposed upon the people by their environment, the archaeologist can build a theoretical model. This model begins with the known facts, adds in the advantages a particular environment offered to man, considers the environmental limitations, and attempts to interpret all of this in terms of an ongoing, living culture.

The tools are known; their functions are determined from their edge wear and associations, sources are known for the raw materials used or worked at the site; the charcoal gives a date and tree species found in that area; and the geology is known. Knowing all of these facts and ranges of possible conditions, the prime requisites of life must be found within their territory once the boundaries of the territory are approximated.

While all of these data are presented from 6LF21 and a tidy picture of a typical day in the life of Paleo-Indian could be drawn, the usefulness of the model must be gauged by its application. Does it fit the data from nearby sites? Can it be used to locate other Paleo-Indian sites? Can deductions be made which are testable and which will provide further insights? These questions can only be answered through future excavations.

Environmental reconstructions for Paleo-Indian sites have been attempted through the use of floral (seeds, pollen, and wood) and faunal (bones) remains. Until very recently these materials have not been available from actual Paleo-Indian habitation sites. Preserved seeds, pollen, wood, and bone from bogs and other contexts in the general vicinity of camp sites have been analyzed. The use of environmental indicators from locations other than actual occupation sites may give a very general view of the environment but not a specific view of man's immediate surroundings. The reason for this displacement was that Paleo-Indian sites either had not yielded appropriate environmental indicators in definite association with man or that the data had not been widely reported. Now all of that will change.

Lisa Fagan's review of pollen diagrams from southern New England (1978:70-92) shows that a tundra existed from 15,000 to 12,000 B.P., a forest-tundra from 12,000 to 10,500 B.P., and open spruce woodland from 10,500 to 9500 B.P., and a coniferous-deciduous forest from 9500 to 7000 B.P. Thus, Paleo-Indians at

6LF21 should have been living in a forest-tundra that was gradually changing to an open spruce woodland. The only problem with this generalization is that it does not take into consideration the range of variation due to localized factors which would permit man and red oak and juniper or white cedar to be found in association at 6LF21.

A similar situation was noted within the Paleo-Indian component at the Shawnee-Minisink site near the Delaware Water Gap in eastern Pennsylvania. J.C. Bernabo and T. Webb (1977) summarized the vegetation in that vicinity as being pine dominated until 9000 B.P. when an oak-dominated deciduous forest began to encroach. Barbara Kauffman and Joseph Dent (1978) do not agree with pine domination being typical of this site with its Paleo-Indian dates of approximately 10,600 B.P., since they excavated carbonized seeds of *Chenopodium* (lambsquarter, goosefoot), *Phytolacca* (pokeweed), grape, *Amaranthus* (pigweed), smartweed, blackberry, hawthorne plum, hackberry, *Lactuca* (wild lettuce),*Physalis* (groundcherry), and sedge. These plants are more typically found in a damp, sunny wood's edge.

Pollen profiles dating to the time of Paleo-Indian have occasionally shown the presence of oak, but it was dismissed as a mere contaminant from the downward movement of pollen from subsequent layers, or from a statistical aberration reflecting the decline in other types of pollen and not a true increase in the amount of oak (Eisenberg 1978:17-35). There are other factors at work: pine produces more pollen than oak. Pine pollen is more likely to be preserved in a bog environment than deciduous tree pollen. But the most important factor to remember is that the palynologist is attempting to reconstruct the dominant vegetational sequence to make generalizations concerning the environment. The archaeologist, on the other hand, should not lose sight of the fact that since man does not live "in general", but in a specific location at a given time, a general statement is not good enough.

In addition to the environmental picture drawn from the direct association of ecofacts with artifacts, pollen profiles from bogs close to Paleo-Indian sites, and geological evidence on glacial or periglacial activities, preserved animal remains also provide important clues. The only unequivocable association of faunal remains at a Paleo-Indian site in the Northeast is fish bones at Shawnee-Minisink in eastern Pennsylvania (Kauffman and Dent 1978). The caribou bones at Dutchess Quarry Cave in eastern New York may or may not have been in association with the fluted point (Guilday 1969). Despite the presence of numerous mammoth and mastodon finds in Connecticut or closeby - the Hillstead mastodon in Farmington, Connecticut (Cook 1978) and the Lake Kitchawan mastodon in Pound Ridge,

37

New York (Weignad 1979), to name the most complete, there have been no proved associations of their bones with man (Dragoo 1979, Ritchie 1965; Fig. 6, Kraft 1973:60).

Because of the association of fluted points with mammoths in the Western United States (Wormington 1964, Jennings 1974: Fig. 3.6), it was assumed that man in the Eastern United States would also have hunted them or their relatives, the mastodons. The distribution of known Paleo-Indian sites and fluted point finds overlaps that of the mammoth and mastodon finds in the Northeast, seemingly giving man access to the beasts. There are only two unsettling aspects to this logical arrangement: the lack of associated remains and their dates.

The absence of fluted points or other artifacts here in direct association with mammoth or mastodon skeletons or butchering marks on their bones can be explained by the vagaries of preservation. The animals are found in bogs or underwater where their bones have not been subjected to the extremely acidic soil common to the Northeast, to the scavenging of other animals, and to the extremes of heat and cold. Since the most frequently found bones are teeth, it is not unexpected that butchering evidence would be rare. Although man would find it to his advantage to drive the animals into a bog where they would be mired and easily slaughtered, there is no evidence that man drove them to the bogs, or butchered the purposely or accidently mired animals, and since their bones would not be likely to be found at occupation sites subjected to bone destroying conditions, there is no direct evidence that they were hunted. While it is obvious that hungry hunters would not pass up the opportunity to make a single kill which would feed a band for weeks, they may not have had the opportunity.

As more carbon-14 dates are received from human occupations and for mammoths and mastodons, the likelihood increases that man was occupying the East close to or after the time of these animals' extinction. With most Paleo-Indian dates more recent than 8500 B.C. (excepting Dutchess Quarry Cave) and the paucity of mammoth/mastodon dates subsequent to 8000 B.C. (Funk 1972:11), the possibility is raised that man did not have much time to hunt them before they disappeared.

Very closely related to this is the reason for their extinction. If man actually slaughtered them, there should be skeletal evidence. If it were an environmental change that forced them from this region and man was occupying the territory they had abandoned because of the advent of new types of vegetation to which they could not adapt, the associated skeletal evidence would be very scant. The second alternative does explain the presence of skeletal evidence as well as the absence of associations with man's tenure in the same region. But, it

38

does not prove they were not contemporaries. Since no one knows for sure the dietary habits of mammoths and mastodons, their proved association with glacial and peri-glacial climates may be misleading. If they were able to adapt to an encroaching deciduous forest, man should have encountered them. If they were not able to adapt and had left the oak areas that man was occupying, precisely what game was man hunting?

Modern oak forests abound with small game from chipmunk size to deer and bear. While bones of larger animals are more likely to have been preserved, those of smaller animals would surely have disintegrated during the past 10,000 years. Even bones of large animals broken to extract the marrow could not be expected to have endured.

Because Paleo-Indian had been stereotyped as "The Big Game Hunter" ever since the fluted points were found in bison and mammoth kills in the West, archaeologists had assumed the same types of fluted points in the East were used for the same large game. When the excavations failed to reveal extensive skeletal remains, poor preservation was cited as the "obvious" cause. This line of reasoning could be fallacious. It was only through the extensive use of flotation at Shawnee-Minisink and 6LF21 that seeds, bones, and bits of charcoal used in making an environmental reconstruction were recovered. Had this procedure been applied as diligently at all other Paleo-Indian excavations, the dietary evidence of Paleo-Indian food gathering and small game hunting might be more extensive.

The evidence as it stands does not disprove the theory of prehistoric elephant hunters in the East, nor does it prove it. The only hard evidence is that man was living at a time close to the extinction of the mammoth and mastodon in the Northeast and that the environment at two of man's camp sites is not known to have been favorable to the beasts. At the same time the picture slowly being developed is that man was living in an econiche with a much more diverse food supply than was thought previously to be the case.

The direct evidence of fish bones and a large variety of edible seeds and plants attests to the fact that man did not live by mammoth alone. He had the ability to obtain and utilize a very diverse array of plants and animals. The time has come to destroy the stereotypes and to collect the solid data needed to show that man was adapting differently in different regions and at different times.

The point will be raised again, but it is important that its ramifications be understood. There are many similarities among all Paleo-Indian sites and artifacts, but each has its own unique aspects. While many of the conclusions drawn from one site are applicable to others, crucial exceptions will be uncovered. In this instance the previously held environmental and dietary assumptions have been attacked with new data and should be reconsidered by future researchers before they are ever applied again.

DESCRIPTIONS OF ARTIFACTS

Rather than present the artifact observations made during the analysis separately from the conclusions and conjecture, they have been combined. The artifact categories (fluted point, graver, utilized flake, etc.) were based upon the morphological traits of the working edges, of stage of manufacture, or of entire specimen as it applies to a general recognized functional type. While the apparent functions of the artifact discussed may be inferred from their names, these can be misleading. The functional attributes of each specimen are discussed in terms of the nature of the motor habits of the people while the artifact was in use, rather than attempt to determine precisely the use of each one. The technical nomenclature used is depicted in Fig. 11.

Probably the most difficult artifact category to understand is bifaces, whether they were discarded in process (rejects) or whether they were completed. This is the first category to be discussed.

Bifacial Rejects and Cores (Plates 5,6; Tables 5,6)

The basic definition of a biface is any stone artifact which has been worked on both faces and along a common edge. For the purpose of this analysis the definition has been expanded to include only those artifacts which exhibit the manufacturing steps of bifacial technology. This would exclude waste flakes which had been retouched on an edge from both laterals. An inspection of the bifacial rejects and core remnants (Plates 5,6) will reveal that extensive flaking has been done not only along the laterals but also across the faces of each specimen. The stages in their production and causes for rejection are discussed in detail.

Tables 5,6 are a metrical and attribute summary of these categories of artifacts. In general there is extreme metric variation in length, width, thickness, weight, and edge angles. The cross sections tend to have at least one convex and one plano face, biconvex and biplano do occur, but concave/convex doesn't. Causes for rejection by the knapper include overshot, material flaws, step fractures, hinge fractures, longitudinal fractures, and combinations of these. At first glance, there seems to be very little similarity within the group. This is deceiving for several reasons.

The first reason for lack of similarity is that these are not finished artifacts. While the technology being employed in their manufacture is the same, the end product is not on view. The end product was never achieved because the knapper never finished. He discarded an unfinished chunk. There is no reason they should be metrically similar.

The similarity present is in the techniques of manufacture, not in the physical resemblance of specimens. The edge angle of the left lateral nearly always corresponds to that of the right. This indicates that the biface was being thinned symmetrically prior to rejection. The flaking on the laterals and across the faces was proceeding on the entire specimen simultaneously, not one section at a time. The exceptions and possible rationales for this are discussed below. The absence of concave faces shows that these are truly bifaces being made from blanks and not just waste flakes being chipped on the margins. The convexity arises because the lateral thinning leaves a medial hump. This hump is gradually and successively reduced by the removal of medial thinning flakes. Had this been a flake, the ventral surface would very likely have been concave and remained that way because of the thinness of flakes.

The technology and techniques for biface production are well illustrated, explained, and discussed by Errett Callahan (1979). His meticulous study through years of careful experimentation documents the stages in biface manufacture, tools of the knapper, selection of appropriate raw materials, the successes, and the tell-tale signs of failure.

Beginning with the premise that Paleo-Indian lithic technology followed approximately the same steps (but not necessarily in the same sequence) from region to region, analysis of the bifacially worked specimens from 6LF21 was undertaken to determine their stage of manufacture and the causes for rejection. According to Callahan, there are five stages in bifacial reduction: obtaining the blank, initial edging, primary thinning, secondary thinning, and final shaping (1979: Table 1). A carefully selected core is boldly flaked to remove the cortex (if present) and to start the process of lateral and longitudinal symmetry. The third step is to remove the medial humps, regularize the lateral flaking, and make the flake scars contact in the center thus adding to its symmetry. The last two steps are the final shaping and sharpening prior to fluting. The trend to be aware of in this procedure is toward increasing thinness, increasing symmetry, and increasingly smaller flakes being removed. Each step can be documented by the nature of the flake scars, as well as the remaining problem areas: asymmetry, inappropriate thickness, medial humps, and assorted fractures.

While museums and site reports are filled with depictions of Paleo-Indian success, a study of their failures is frequently more instructive. A study of failures shows the sequence of manufacture, the causes for rejection, the number of obstacles which are faced in achieving lithic excellence, and the knappers tenacity to proceed despite a high risk of failure.

The reasons for bifaces breaking in unexpected and unwanted ways are clearly outlined and illustrated by Callahan: step and hinge fractures, lateral and longitudinal fractures, an attempt to remove too much material with one blow, overshot during lateral or end thinning, and/or material flaws. Each one can be caused by a variety of circumstances and not cause an immediate fracture, but merely set the stage for future rejection in subsequent thinning attempts.

A step fracture is a nearly vertical, abrupt break which occurs when a thick mass of stone is encountered in the course of removing a flake. The blow was not sufficient to carry the force through the resistant mass, so the flake terminated abruptly. Hinge fractures are similar in that the mass was encountered, but the force carried upward leaving a flake scar on the top of an abrupt break. Rejection will occur if there is no way to remove that mass of stone from another direction. Another blow directed from the same place as the first will either not be strong enough to carry through the mass, thereby deepening the step, or it will be so powerful that too much material will be removed causing a fracture and definite rejection.

The attempt to remove too much material with one blow may cause fractures laterally or longitudinally, depending upon the weaknesses in the stone and the amount of material previously removed from different sections. The resulting fracture can be parallel or perpendicular to the flake being removed. Even if no obvious medial humps or other problem areas exist on the biface, a blow removing too large a flake can cause fracturing just because of the size of the flake removed.

Knowing this, why would anyone purposely attempt to strike off more than they know is possible? Of course it happens accidentally for several reasons. A blow too far above the medial line of the edge of the biface, a striking platform prepared too high above the medial line, or a striking angle which is too straight or shallow will cause the removal of too much material. This can be a cause of overshot when a very large, thick flake is detached, leaving a deep scar across a face or a concavity on one lateral. Very large, thick flakes can be removed early during core preparation because there is sufficient mass in the stone to dissipate the force of the blow. The amount of force which can be effectively dissipated rapidly decreases as the blank is thinned.

Overshot can occur at any time in thinning from the sides or from either end. The attempted removal of medial thinning flakes and true channel flakes must proceed with extreme caution because the blank has been markedly thinned by this time. The knapper knows from experience that a single channel flake may not remove enough of the medial section, but that several individual flakes must be driven to avoid the inevitable fracture from trying to remove too much material at one time.

Material flaws observed in this collection included different colored and textured flint on either side of a contact zone. Causes of differences in color and texture are impurities in the flint, different rates of cooling or times of intrusion into the original rock, and weathering. The result is that the flint is not homogeneous. Were it homogeneous, any force applied to it would be dissipated predictably. The presence of differences from any source will cause unpredictable reactions. A contact zone within the flint can weaken the stone so much that it can be broken with your bare hands.

If these material flaws are not evident on the surface of the stone, which is very likely with cobbles and less likely with quarried chunks, biface manufacture could have proceeded quite far before the unavoidable snap. Because of the tremendous shocks and pressures during tool manufacturing, it seems highly improbable that bifaces with material flaws could have been produced only to break during use. A biface with a material flaw supposedly broken during use should be examined very closely to determine that it was really a completed artifact and not simply a tool in process.

Callahan had a tremendous advantage in his analysis of bifacial tool manufacture that the archaeological researcher can seldom hope to have: all of the pieces to the puzzle. The modern flintknapper knows exactly when something goes wrong by the broken biface in his hand. By putting all of the pieces back together he can show exactly the sequence of steps leading to the demise of his replications. Although fitting fragments were found at this site from four different bifaces or their flakes, more work of this nature has to be done to reconstruct precise manufacturing steps from the actual detritus. Because of this, the current analysis and interpretation of bifacial rejects will attempt to explain the most likely cause(s) for rejection rather than pinpointing the sole, definitive mistake. If Callahan is correct, the clues to cause(s) of failure are still present even if all of the pieces are not.

One reason for spending so much time with bifacial rejects is that the point has to be made emphatically that these are rejects and that there is a very good possibility that many (most?) of what are being cataloged as projectile point tips, bases, midsections, blanks, or blades are not completed specimens. A reject is a reject and not a completed artifact. When they are recognized for what they are, archaeological interpretations will be far more precise. Closely related to this is the explanation for a seemingly good biface not being used because it was "lost", "cached for future use", or "forgotten". A determination should be made first that it was actually a completed specimen and not one with insurmountable flaws which no manner of lithic expertise could overcome. Although the collection analyzed was Paleo-Indian, the problem of reject interpretation applies to all time periods.

The absence of Stage 1 bifaces (unmodified chunks of high grade flint) is to be expected at any non-quarry site. Their presence would suggest not only a nearby flint source, but also a reserve supply of lithic material brought to the camp for future use. A brief walk along the river banks adjacent to the excavation in 1977 did yield small water-polished flint cobbles. This raises the possibility discussed in more detail elsewhere that a source for some (all?) of the flint from this site was derived from the Shepaug River in the form of water-polished cobbles.

A single Stage 2 biface (Plate 6c) was found in two pieces more than 15m apart. This tabular core was roughly flaked on the dorsal face to remove all of the cortex. A single large, thin flake removed more than 66% of the water-polished cortex on the ventral face. Although separate longitudinal flakes were struck to remove cortex on both laterals, only one was completely decorticated. Initial flaking on the distal end removed the cortex and left a very ragged edge. Despite battering on the proximal end, all of the water-polished cortex remains.

The apparent cause for rejection was a severe step fracture located one-third of the distance between the distal and proximal ends. The flake precipitating the step fracture was too thick and caused a longitudinal fracture perpendicular to the step when the force of the blow encountered the central mass of the core. No subsequent flaking was attempted on either piece of the core.

A Stage 2 biface (Plate 6a) consisting of three fitting fragments was totally decorticated with no remnant humps or ridges. The edge had been centered on approximately 50% of the specimen, with edge angles reduced to between 40 and 50 degrees. The half lacking the centered edges has deep concavities.

The reason for rejection was a longitudinal fracture caused by a blow intended to remove a thinning flake. Only half of the flake scar with half of the prepared striking platform is extant. Callahan (1979: Fig. 41d-f) obtained the same results attempting to end-thin a biface using a punch.

Although this Stage 3 biface (Plate 6b) bears an overall physical resemblance to the previously discussed one and to the one pictured by Callahan (41d), the reason for rejection is more difficult to pinpoint. The edge has been centered on most of the artifact with edge angles approximating 40°. Despite the prominent medial hump, secondary flaking of the lateral has occurred.

The small flake scars from a hinge fracture abutting the hump suggest that an attempt to remove it from the far edge met with resistance, resulting in a lateral break perpendicular to the hinge. The hinge fracture associated with the medial hump might not have been the primary reason for fracture, but merely the blow dislodging a previously weakened segment of the biface.

This is an excellent illustration of the advantage an experimental archaeologist has compared to a researcher working with 10,000-year-old evidence. Callahan was able to state convincingly the cause for a fracture because he was carefully observing each phase of the manufacturing process. By being able to completely reconstruct a core from all of its flakes, he knew when a single blow weakened a segment that later dislodged with subsequent blows.

A Stage 3 biface (Plate 5f) exhibits two lateral snaps because of material flaws. The flaws are seen as narrow, twisting veins in the dorsal and ventral faces. Had the stone been homogeneous, the shock waves from the detachment blow would have been evenly dissipated.

The four remaining Stage 3 bifaces (Plate 5) are lateral fragments having edge angles between 40° and 65°, erratic edge symmetry, and incomplete medial thinning. Wide, incomplete flake scars would have extended beyond the fractured lateral to the medial section of the biface. Two bifaces in particular (Plate 5a, b) clearly evidence overshot as the prime reason for rejection. The other two (Plate 5d, e) have flake scars which could be attributed to overshot or to thinning attempts which met resistance and caused the fracture. If the conjoining pieces were examined, they would show either the long, wide scars characteristic of overshot or hinge fracture evidence.

A Stage 4 biface (Plate 5j) was worked to edge-centered symmetry with edge angles of nearly 35°, but without secondary lateral retouch. The reason for rejection was end-thinning overshot identical to Callahan's replication using an antler billet (1979:132, Fig. 59a). In assessing the cause for rejecting his biface, Callahan (p. 147) cites excessive platform isolation and a blow which was directed too straight in, as well as being improperly elevated.

Two Stage 4 bifaces (Plate 5c, k) resemble projectile point tips but can be recognized for what they really are under closer examination.

45

The large flake scars lacking secondary retouch, asymmetry, and lateral fractures caused by a blow from the base are clues that these are unfinished rejects.

The cause for rejection was overshot during end thinning. Because end thinning occurs repeatedly at different stages of biface manufacture, it is difficult to determine if the intention was to thin the medial section or to actually flute the biface. If the single unfinished fluted point from the site can be used as a "typical" specimen the occupants were making, the overshot probably occurred during a thinning attempt. A true flute would not have come so close to the tip, nor have been so deep. Looking at the same data from a different perspective, one could say that this was an ill-conceived fluting attempt. The intended channel flake carried too far and too deeply, causing the fracture. Were the remainder of the biface extant, an analysis could determine more precisely the typical manufacturing steps in use at this site. As it is, the one nearly finished fluted point (Plate 7b) will have to stand as "typical" of their procedures.

The two remaining Stage 4 bifaces (Plate 5g, i) have edge angles between 35° and 50° associated with prominent medial humps, secondary bifacial thinning, and the absence of bi-convex symmetry. The combination of Stage 3 and Stage 4 traits is undoubtedly due to repeated attempts to remove the medial humps.

The reason for rejection in each case was a hinge fracture. The probable cause for the hinge fracture on one specimen (Plate 5i) is overshot or an attempt to remove too much material with a single blow. One face shows a single shallow flake scar covering nearly 50% of the surface. A second one is deeper but covers 33% of the surface. On the other face is another very large scar extending to the hinge (and probably beyond prior to the fracture), which has a very deep negative bulb of percussion. Since neither is complete and the conjoining fragments are missing, it is impossible to determine the sequence of their removal.

As Callahan has stated previously in different contexts, the likelihood of failure in biface manufacture is increased markedly with the size, depth, and force employed to detach any flake. The previously discussed specimen illustrated this point well. At Stage 4 the knapper should not be removing flakes with the powerful blows that leave prominent bulbs of percussion or leave huge, deep flake scars.

A Stage 5 biface (Plate 5h) had been symmetrically trimmed with centered edges, edge angles of 27° to 45°, and secondary retouching, but the knapper had certain flaws to overcome. There was an attempt to recover from a previous step fracture, but this did not lead to rejection. The lateral snap resulted from an unsuccessful end-thinning attempt that encountered a material flaw. The flaw is obvious on the fracture plane but not on the dorsal or ventral faces.

The application of Callahan's criteria for recognizing the reasons and causes for biface rejection prior to completion provides reasonable explanations fitting the observable evidence. While all of these explanations should not necessarily be taken as conclusive, since all of the broken fragments of a given biface were not present, characteristics used in defining the stages of biface reduction and in recognizing certain types of fractures and their causes will prevent the careful researcher from incorrectly portraying rejects as retouched knives; projectile point tips, bases, or midsections; or scrapers. This type of careful analysis coupled with edge wear studies will clearly show that lateral or longitudinal snaps during manufacture are very different from the breaks occurring after an impact of a projectile point with a bone.

A familiarity with Paleo-Indian biface production may even lead to a reconsideration of the importance of debitage analysis in surface collections. Clues to Paleo-Indian sites may lie in an ability to recognize their debitage and rejects from those of other groups. The same may be true of each other culture in a given region.

Closely related to the problem of misidentifying rejects as broken, finished artifacts, are misinterpretations of the manufacturing process. Although there is variation in the sequential steps of biface reduction, the idea of fluting being the final step has died hard. The specimen from this site (Plate 7b) is evidence that this is not the final step.

A second misinterpretation of manufacturing procedures is not in the sequence but in the procedure. Floyd Painter suggested that the snapped-off bases were actually an intentional part of the manufacturing process of bifaces at the Williamson Site. "The blank was then pressed flat against an anvil of wood or stone, with the basal end projecting about one-quarter of an inch (7mm) over the edge of the anvil. A sharp blow of the hammerstone delivered at right angles to the blank served to break or 'snap-off' a short section of the basal end" (1974:24). He also stated that fluting was accomplished by placing the blank on an anvil and striking a bone, antler, or ivory punch with a hammerstone.

Callahan's experimental replications refute these procedures (1979:19-20). Basal snapping in the manner outlined would result in a different type of break that would not be as clean and sharp as the ones evidenced. While this type of snapping may occur in far thinner specimens, the likelihood of unpredictable results would preclude the use of this procedure in bifacial reduction. The use of an anvil for a rest while fluting would severely damage the tip and could lead to further knapping problems or rejection. Although the detractors of replication argue that the similarity in finished products does not necessarily prove that the same techniques were used prehistorically, they have to admit that the laws of physics, the basic raw materials, and the manufacturing implements have not changed.

The utility of replication in archaeology is not to make modern look-alikes, but to demonstrate that certain procedures will consistently produce the same results. The prehistoric knapper, as well as any craftsman working in any media, knows he must have predictability in his raw materials. They had to consistently apply those techniques which produced predictable results. They would probably be able to take advantage of the occasional serendipitous break, but that is not what gets the tools made.

After reading Callahan's most recent work (1979), I tackled the problem of bifacially worked specimens differently than I would have had I never read it. As a matter of fact, reading Callahan has totally changed my perspective on "projectile point tips, bases, and midsections". I cringe to think of the hundreds of these bifacially worked pieces which were actually rejects because of breakage during the knapping process, which were cataloged and reported as parts of finished projectile points. For anyone who hasn't seen the book, you are still suffering under a delusion of ages past. He outlines in exhaustive detail the procedures for making bifaces and what the mess looks like when you do it wrong. He leaves little doubt about the nature of biface manufacture and its by-products.

Since rejects were tools in progress before they broke beyond salvage, a description of them should have some bearing upon the final product. Unfortunately, this study could not include such a comparison since there were no finished flint bifaces. The miniature points were made from flakes which were bifacially retouched rather than being manufactured from a bifacially reduced core.

Fluted Point (Plate 7, Table 7)

The single fluted point (Plate 7b) was found as two fitting segments. As is discussed in the section on bifacial rejects, the uncompleted specimens are more instructive of manufacturing techniques than the completed ones. This projectile point is no exception. Not only does it illustrate the knapper's craft, but also his skill and confidence when confronted with apparent rejection.

If a modern knapper were to examine this point, he would be struck immediately by many contradictions. The basal half is a Stage 5 biface with the edge symmetry, retouching, and fluting indicative of a nearly completed projectile point. Closer retouching of the laterals and basal grinding are needed to complete it.

However, the other half is somewhere between a Stage 2 and Stage 5 biface. Although all of the cortex has been removed, a strong medial hump, step fractures, rudimentary edging, and large flake scars still remain on a fluted biface. These contradictions do not necessarily imply that the knapper had planned to work one section of the biface to completion before working on the remainder. This is the result, but it was probably not the plan.

The knapper was faced with a series of ultimately overwhelming obstacles which, had they been overcome, would have truly represented the ultimate in knapping expertise. A clue to the primary problem is the marked contrast in color and texture obvious on the dorsal and ventral faces. The abrupt changes are indicative of contact zones between different types of flint, which could have resulted from non-contemporaneous igneous intrusions having different impurities, rates of cooling, or other factors precluding homogeneity. The most obvious color differences are on either side of the fracture. Other material flaws are highlighted by the light-colored streaks on the basal half.

These types of material flaws make a particular piece of stone extremely difficult to work because it lacks homogeneity, causing the stone to break unpredictably. When the force of the flake-detaching blow travels through the stone and encounters varying amounts of resistance, erratic breaks can occur. Existing stress cracks can cause the shock waves to travel anywhere but where the knapper intended. Second guessing the non-obvious, I think the fluting or medial thinning was done prior to the edge thinning. At this point the material flaws would have been obvious to the knapper. If the fluting were to succeed, the relatively minor edge thinning could be done later.

The base of the biface was prepared for fluting by the removal on either face of two small flakes between the ears. This is not the Enterline Fluting Technique described by Witthoft (1952) where long guide flutes were supposedly driven on either side of and prior to the actual channel flake. These flakes are far too short and narrow and terminate between one-third and one-half the distance to the first step fracture.

The ventral face (without the catalog number) has two step fractures and a hinge fracture in the flute. The first flute carried to the hinge fracture closest to the tip but was too shallow. A second flute was struck to deepen the groove but terminated in a step fracture. The third attempt removed most of the scars from the first two but ended two-thirds of the distance to the break along the first flaw line. Although subsequent flutes could not have been driven without losing a portion of the basal concavity thus shortening the point, a large medial hump remained near the tip.

The dorsal face may have been fluted by the removal of two separate flakes. The remnant of a very shallow, narrow groove extends beyond a hinge fracture in the deeper, wider groove. Shallow ripple marks in the groove demonstrate that resistance was encountered by the shock waves when passing over the flaw lines and again when crossing into the different colored zone.

None of the channel (medial thinning?) flakes from the site exhibit the traits seen in these flutes. Most of the flakes are of a different colored flint. They lack a striking platform having the thick bulb of percussion which would correspond to the deep negative bulb in these flutes. The flutes from the point would have to be thinner than the channel flakes found elsewhere at the site. The flute on the ventral face is narrower than any of the distal or medial channel flake segments. The proximal flakes are too short to fit. Not only do the channel flakes not physically fit into the flutes of the projectile point, they seem to have very different attributes.

The discrepancies between the flutes and the channel flakes should not cause one to doubt their contemporaneity or to start searching for the "missing" channel flakes to fit the flutes or the "other" fluted points from which the channel flakes came. Rather it is further evidence that all channel flakes did not come from flutes. The removal of medial thinning flakes does occur at other stages in the manufacturing process than just fluting.

The second reason for rejection would be the tip. A single flake driven from left lateral carried too far and too deep (overshot) in an attempt to remove the large hump on the ventral face. As if the short flutes and overshot tip were not enough of a problem to the knapper, a major step fracture near the tip on the ventral right lateral could not have been ignored without altering the type of tool being made. An experienced knapper would have realized that this was an obvious reason for rejection or for making a different specimen from this biface. It will be demonstrated that this person did not reject the unfinished biface due to these three reasons, nor did he start working on his second choice.

The ultimate reason for rejection was the transverse fracture splitting the nearly finished biface into two large pieces and several tinier ones which were not recovered. The reason for the fracture was material flaws exacerbated by the attempted removal of too much material in a single blow that met resistance and failed to carry consistently through the non-homogeneous material.

Pinpointing the precise flake which was the ultimate cause is more difficult. The likely culprit was struck from the ventral left lateral starting on the basal side of the fracture, extending across the fracture, and hitting the hump. A deep stress crack and sharp, close ripple marks characterize the excessive resistance that this flake encountered. While it is conceivable that a nearly full-length channel flake could have been removed and simultaneously caused a midpoint transverse snap, it is likely that was merely a factor in weakening the stone and setting up the final break for a subsequent flake.

The preceding has been a discussion of four "fatal" reasons for rejection on a single biface. Any one of them would have been sufficient reason to reject, but the knapper continued. Although the events leading to final rejection cannot be accurately reconstructed without all of the fitting flakes to determine their sequence of detachment, the following conjecture is presented in an attempt to explain the multi-stage nature of the incomplete specimen and the presence of four reasons for discarding a biface which could not be completed.

The close retouch on the basal half of the specimens shows that the basic outline of the finished biface was to have been very nearly as it appears in Plate 7b with the exception of the missing tip. Although additional close retouch is needed to complete the edge symmetry and add a more regular pattern to the flakes for sharpness, the removal of major lateral thinning flakes was not planned.

The extant fluting was done after the basic outline and the major lateral and end thinning had been completed. Subsequent to the fluting, shallow, narrow lateral flakes were driven to intersect the flute to further refine the edges, thin the laterals, and to decrease the edge angles. Many small flakes terminating at or near the sides of the actual flutes characterize this procedure.

Despite the fluting, the biface had not been completely thinned to remove the large humps to the left and directly in front of the groove. The attempt to remove the hump from the right lateral resulted in a step fracture caused by too shallow a striking angle. The knapper could not recover from this error by building another striking platform in the same place and adjusting the striking angle. This would have resulted in narrowing the biface so much on one side that it would no longer be symmetrical. The only way to correct that asymmetry would be to re-trim all of the laterals. It is also doubtful that a second flake struck from the same place could have removed that much material without causing a lateral break.

The knapper attempted to resolve this difficulty by removing a thick portion from the left lateral nearer the tip. This maneuver resulted in an intentional overshot that did not carry far enough across the ventral face to remove the hump.

The next attempt to remove the medial hump was to strike a flute. Although the flute would had to have carried nearly to the tip to

51

remove the hump, this does not mean that the groove would have remained in the finished specimen. More lateral thinning and reduction of edge angles would have obliterated any trace of the furthest extent of the flute. Since the flute did not succeed in removing the hump entirely, further flaking was done and resulted in the fracture. Had the flute succeeded in removing the hump, the problem of asymmetry could have been resolved.

Knapping attempts are the definite cause of the transverse fractures. Callahan (1979:20) discusses why other possible explanations for breaking such as dropping, snapping between thumbs and forefingers, and stepping on them are not really likely to be at fault.

The reasons for the breaking of this particular biface have been examined in great detail not only to show the stubbornness of the knapper in the face of repeated challenges and his skill in overcoming incomplete (short) flutes, steep step fractures, severe material flaws, a decided change in the size of the originally intended biface, but also to hypothesize as to why he bothered after the first setback. The skill shown reflects his experience, but by the same token should have shown him the likelihood of failure. Why did he continue: self-confidence due to years of experience, a desperate need for a projectile point with no time for starting from scratch, a shortage of raw material? To resolve this argument I suggest a bottle of wine, a tray of cheese and crackers, three friends with differing backgrounds, and several hours to spend.

Miniature Points (Plate 7, Table 7)

Of the four miniature points recognized in the collection, two "completed" ones are more similar to one another than either of the incomplete ones. A waste flake was selected for one specimen (Plate 7c). When the striking platform was extant, the large "channel flake" was struck, removing part of the dorsal face of the left ear. The basal concavity and laterals were closely retouched unifacially to refine the outline. The lateral fracture at the distal end is a step fracture from the removal of the original flake from the core. In an effort to achieve or maintain symmetry, a small section of the left lateral was not retouched. The marks on the ventral face are a bulb of percussion and a series of broad ripple marks remaining from the flake'sdetachment from the core.

In many respects the second miniature point (Plate 7a) is similar to the first. Both were done on waste flakes, had the original striking platform at the base of the finished point, and had steep retouching to achieve symmetry rather than to prepare the point for utilization.

52

This specimen is slightly different in that it is a bifacially-flaked uniface.

This contradictory term is used to reflect the unifacial nature of the flake's preparation and the bifacial nature of its edge retouch. No attempt was being made to make the cross section biconvex except on the laterals. The ventral face still has the very shallow ripple marks from its detachment from the core. Although most of the perimeter has been flaked on both faces (bifacially), a section of the left lateral was only unifacially flaked. Had it been flaked bifacially, the symmetry would have been lost.

Another specimen has traits of a miniature point in progress (Plate 7d). An attempt was made to make a basal concavity between two projections on the proximal end (striking platform) of a waste flake. This maneuver was only partially successful in isolating a single ear. The subsequent retouching of the laterals of that ear could not remove a large medial hump. The flaking was primarily unifacial except for the right lateral where it was bifacial.

The last of the projectile points in this category (Plate 7e) was included not because it bore a physical resemblance to the others, but because it was made in the same fashion. In this attempt to simulate a biface on a waste flake the striking platform was also at the base. Bilateral bifacial retouching extends nearly to the tip on the left lateral but is absent on the proximal. The proximal end evidences a lateral fracture due to a material flaw where the striking platform had been.

The intended purpose for these specimens is unknown. There are no signs of wear, regularity of retouch to prepare an edge for utilization, or known associations. Ethnographic analogy suggests use as a practice piece, or toy, part of a medicine bundle, or ????? The argument against any of these being practice pieces is that they do not exhibit the same traits or sequence of manufacturing techniques seen in completed or rejected bifaces. If a person were developing the necessary motor habits needed for manufacturing bifaces, he would not practice by unifacially retouching a waste flake.

However, a person wishing a replica (toy) of a true bifacial implement may get the desired outline and effect by selecting an appropriate waste flake and doing relatively simple retouching. Retouching on such thin specimens was probably pressure flaking to assure accurate placement of the tiny flakes. Whether such a replica would be appropriate for a medicine bundle intended for curing, hunting magic to assure a sufficient food supply, or other activities vital to a society's or individual's well-being can only be answered within the context of their culture and not ours.

Reinforcement for the replica or toy function of these miniatures is

53

found by a close comparison of one of them (Plate 7a) to the nearly completed fluted point (Plate 7b). This was the first artifact found at the site other than flint debitage that raised the possibility of a Paleo-Indian occupation. The similarity of this point to previous fluted point finds in the Northeast was striking: the shape of the ears, basal concavity, constriction above the ears, point of maximum width, overall length/width ratio, and delicate retouching could not be ignored. The same traits duplicated in the full-size point are not coincidental. This was a deliberate attempt at a faithful replication, but without the flute.

A possible use for these miniatures is for the archaeologist to obtain further clues in determining manufacturing procedures for bifaces. The placement of the striking platform at the base of the point is one of the consistencies in their manufacture that is a point of debate in biface manufacture. Painter (1974:24) says that the heavier, thicker end of the core was chosen for the tip. This is usually the end having the striking platform or its remnant bulb of percussion. Callahan (1979:14) disagrees, saying that the orientation of the biface may change during manufacture to take advantage of the unique properties of each core and their changes as reduction proceeds.

Because this is a single occupation site, the artifacts exhibit a high degree of similarity. All other Paleo-Indian sites which have a large artifact collection exhibit more variability because they were occupied repeatedly by different groups at different times for possibly different reasons. If bifaces made by these people usually had the extant traces of the striking platform at the base of the finished point, it is possible that replicas of these points would also. The problem of not having more bifaces and their fitting flakes to determine manufacturing procedures makes this highly conjectural.

The miniatures are in a class by themselves at this site and are extremely rare in Paleo-Indian collections in the rest of the Eastern United States. These are positively not full-sized, completed bifaces which were resharpened and reduced. They are bilaterally and bifacially retouched waste flakes that are more similar to unifaces in manufacture than bifaces. Other so-called miniature points lack the thinness, symmetry, and deliberate retouch best seen in Plate 7a. Kraft (1973:76 Plate 2c, d) has similar specimens from the Plenge site which are as short, but much wider.

Having said this, I know that I am opening a Pandora's box because the key word is "Paleo-Indian". When these specimens were first exhibited at the American Indian Archaeological Institute, a local collector showed me a slightly larger, near duplicate of the best of the miniature points. He had found his specimen years ago at a site which had no evidence of having a Paleo-Indian component. Since

54

then, other people from Western Connecticut have also come forward with similar finds at supposedly non-Paleo-Indian sites. The overall similarities in these specimens suggest a regionally meaningful diagnostic trait, if they can actually be proved to be from Paleo-Indian sites. The definition of a Paleo-Indian site was discussed above and is crucial to this dilemma of a possible diagnostic trait which has been previously unrecognized. Now that these points have been identified at a single Paleo-Indian site, future finds in the absence of diagnostic Paleo-Indian artifacts should be considered very carefully. Not every miniature will be a Paleo-Indian artifact but a careful analysis of associated debitage and other artifacts should be done before writing off a possible Paleo-Indian site because a fluted point has not been found (yet).

Channel Flakes (Plates 8, 9, Tables 8, 9)

The metrical and attribute summary of each channel flake from the excavation reveals certain consistencies. While there is a degree of variation, most of the specimens are convex-plano in longitudinal and lateral cross section; lack a bulb of percussion or evidence of significant ripple marks or stress cracks; have very acute edge angles; are widest between the midpoint and the distal end; and are about the same thickness. Transverse flaking and extensive grinding (abrading) were used to make relatively narrow striking platforms. Distal and proximal ends (only distal for those having an extant striking platform) exhibit a clean, nearly vertical step fracture as opposed to an acute, gently sloping hinge fracture. Five (Plates 8a-e) bear evidence of previous medial thinning or fluting attempts, and four others (Plate 9) have been utilized. These observations must be discussed in detail to understand their significance.

The most frequently posed questions in interpreting channel flakes are (1) how long were they when initially struck from the biface, (2) if they broke, was this purposeful or accidental, and (3) where are the other fluted points? I would like to reply by saying that these are probably the wrong questions to ask because the nature of channel flakes is misunderstood.

The underlying problem is that all so-called channel flakes were not struck to flute a biface. The term medial thinning flake would be more descriptive of the reason for most so-called channel flakes being struck at all. Only the flakes actually resulting in a flute should be called channel flakes. The problem precluding a strict adherence to this rule is recognizing channel flakes and medial thinning flakes for what they really are.

During the reduction of cores to bifaces, many thinning flakes have to be struck. Bifacial thinning flakes were struck from the lateral toward the central axis of the biface to make a symmetrical blank. Since these flakes did not carry the entire distance across the face, a medial ridge was created. This ridge bears flake scars from thinning flakes driven from either lateral. To thin the central part of the biface, this medial ridge must be removed from either the distal or proximal end of the blank. Because bifacial thinning cannot remove a great mass of material in a single blow or the likelihood of fracture leading to rejection is increased, successive medial thinning flakes must be driven to thin the blank. Only the last of the medial thinning flakes is the channel flake that leaves the characteristic groove in fluted points. Several channel flakes may be required to achieve the desired depth and length of fluting.

This does not answer the question of how they broke, but it suggests that there is often a difficulty in deciding if they are really broken. Specimens lacking a striking platform are medial or distal fragments which cannot be extrapolated into complete channel flakes. The problem with proximal fragments (ones with striking platforms) is that the steep step fracture may precisely fit into a completed projectile point groove or it may be far too short. If it is too short, it could still be a complete specimen from a flute made by removing three channel flakes. This dilemma is compounded when the subject of step fracture during manufacture is raised.

The characteristic step in grooves of completed fluted points fits the pattern seen on distal portions of (so-called) channel flakes. The shock waves created by the blow of detachment meet a section of great resistance in the stone and an abrupt fracture results. This explains the distal step fracture, but what about the medial flakes having step fractures on both the distal and proximal ends? While a flake may break into two pieces during removal, the likelihood of the medial break being an abrupt step fracture is extremely small. The question to ask with flakes not having striking platforms is, why were they purposely broken, not how long were they.

Since in the present collection of 15 specimens all four of the utilized flakes lacked striking platforms, the interesting possibility of intentional snapping to make flakes suitable for utilization without further retouch is suggested. While a striking platform may be an advantage with a hand-held implement, it is a marked disadvantage with hafted tools set into a bone or wood handle. While microscopic examination of each utilized channel flake revealed no evidence of hafting, short duration use would not necessarily leave wear marks. Another trait shared by the utilized channel flakes is that they are among the longest of the flakes. The utilized channel flakes do not

56

appear to have been arbitrarily selected for use, nor do they seem to have been intentionally produced for utilization.

The last statement was prompted by the shared attributes of all channel flakes (Tables 8,9). Edge angles are very consistent except where they have been steepened by utilization or damage. Edge angle is a function of the thickness and width of the flake being removed, with consistency of right and left angles a result of symmetrical bifacial thinning. The narrow range of variation from specimen to specimen and edge angle to edge angle strongly suggests that un-utilized channel flakes were produced in the same way and for the same reasons as utilized ones: medial thinning or fluting. A comparison of utilized channel flakes to other utilized flakes shows very little metrical or attribute similarity. Flakes were selected for utilization because they had the necessary attributes for the task at hand and not because they were intentionally produced to be used.

The frequently encountered statement that there are so many channel flakes and so few fluted points can be rebutted simply by saying that not all channel flakes are actually channel flakes. Many are medial thinning flakes. The same answer should also apply when someone asks where the fluted points are that have flutes 4.78cm long: nowhere. Since there are very few fluted points in the literature with flutes that long and the single one from this site was much smaller, the very long channel flakes should be considered to be medial thinning flakes until proved differently.

One of the so-called channel flakes (Plate 8k) does bear a resemblance to the others in certain attributes, but the platform angle of 40° and a close inspection show the similarity to bifacial thinning flakes. The extreme thickness, width, and weight could not be typical of true channel flakes. This amount of material could not have been removed from the medial section of a nearly completed biface without snapping it. Even though it does bear a resemblance to channel flakes, a medial thinning flake should be recognized for what it is, even if it cannot always be differentiated on a case-by-case basis. Knowing that the difference does exist will assist in interpreting Paleo-Indian sites.

Utilized Flakes (Plate 10, Table 9)

The category of utilized flakes does not include all of the specimens which exhibit any utilization, but merely those waste flakes which were utilized without retouching. The waste flake determination is made on the basis of a lack of morphological similarity caused by purposeful flaking to make a specific working edge.

Utilized flakes as a group do have morphological similarities without being physically similar in overall appearance. These morphological similarities arise from the nature of the flake selected for use, the nature of the utilization (edge wear), and the location of the wear. The similarity in the edge wear patterning may or may not be due to the similar functions for which they were utilized. A large variable is the degree of utilization as evidenced by the length of the utilized edge and the presence or absence of continuous vs. discontinuous edge wear.

Utilized flakes are differentiated from retouched flakes as are retouched flakes from finished artifacts, bifacial rejects, and waste flakes. Retouched flakes show evidence of purposeful retouch which has not proceeded to the point that the specimen takes on the recognizable traits of a functionally defined tool category. In other words it is a miscellaneous category having a diversity of specimens. It is often difficult (impossible?) to differentiate between a retouched flake and a utilized one when the only evidence is a worn or flaked lateral.

The nature of utilization evidence must be examined in detail since it is a clue to function. The length of edge wear on a given lateral is important so long as the measurement is of the same type of continuous wear. If the type of wear changes, this could have been caused by a change in function, duration of function during a given task, or multi-functional use for a single task. The angle of edge wear is recorded, as it reflects the duration or intensity of use, although it may not be indicative of function. The edge angle will become less acute as the edge is worn more and more. Since no retouching is being done to enhance the edges, the edge angle at any given moment is only reflecting the amount of use the edge has received. Since the flake scars are actually limited to the edge itself and extend only less than 1.0mm onto the face, a more accurate or meaningful measurement would be the dorsal/ventral face angle.

In order to have been selected for utilization without further retouch, an appropriate waste flake must have had the necessary dorsal/ventral angle for being used for its intended function. Once it had outlived its task or the functional attributes for which it was initially selected, it was reworked or discarded. Subtly reworked utilized flakes could have been re-utilized with no evidence of reworking. Discarded ones being analyzed here may have composite edge wear evidence from different functions or only evidence of the last function they served.

The large number of utilized flakes including utilized channel flakes (Plates 9, 10) suggest that they were "cheap". Waste flakes were abundant. The selection of appropriate ones for use was quicker than making a given tool from a core, and they could be discarded when no longer useful. Additionally, the people were maximizing a scarce resource. Since they were not camped on a flint outcropping, every piece of flint had to be utilized to best advantage. Core reduction or primary flakes were reserved for the projectile points and heavy scrapers. Large flakes were used to make knives, gravers, and graving spurs. Tools which did not have to be made to exacting specifications (general purpose) were much more diverse in overall morphology and were just utilized waste flakes. A flaw in the scarce resources aspect of this theory is the paucity of specialized multiple-function tools. Other collections have implements which look like a Paleo-Indian version of a Swiss Army knife with a scraping edge, multiple gravers, knife edge, and a spokeshave.

The laterals of a sharp flake seem to present themselves as obvious knives. The narrower distal area is more suggestive of a scraper. The proximal end is the least likely for use since the striking platform or its remnant bulb of percussion or heavy ripple marks would have to be removed prior to use. Alternatively, because this was the heaviest area of the entire flake, it could take the most use without showing the wear.

Of all of the utilized flakes only one will be discussed in detail. The remainder are summarized in Table 9 and Plates 9, 10. The one being described in detail is a bifacial reject (Plate 10g, Table 9). This Stage 3 biface was discarded when an attempt to remove the medial hump from the tip and from the right lateral each ended in a step fracture with no hope of further medial thinning without drastically altering the size of the finished artifact. An overshot along the left lateral did not remove the medial hump. The distal break was due in part to material flaws which can be seen on the dorsal face. Rather than discard the bifacial reject, it was utilized.

Scrapers (Plate 11, Table 10)

Of the four scrapers in the collection the spurred sidescraper discussed with the gravers is multi-functional. Of the other three, two are endscrapers and one is a side/endscraper. The scraper designation is warranted by the steep, unifacially retouched edge. The ventral face of each shows minor edge damage in the form of impact fractures with minute negative bulbs of percussion. Mixed in with the retouching on the dorsal face is an unknown amount of edge wear and damage. As the leading edge breaks away during use, the edge angle gets increasingly less acute until the edge is retouched or the scraper is discarded.

The quartz scraper (Plate 11a) is from a level higher than the Paleo-Indian artifacts are usually found but below the Archaic levels. While quartz is not commonly found in Paleo-Indian contexts, its morphological traits are highly similar to those scrapers which are definitely Paleo-Indian.

The side/endscraper (Plate 11c) has a significant remnant of its water-worn, cobble cortex intact on the un-retouched right lateral and dorsal face. A tabular core (Plate 6c) found in the same square has the same type of cobble exterior, banding, and luster. They could have come from the same large cobble.

The thumbnail scraper (Plate 11b) was not excavated during 1977. It was from a 1973 test pit dug in the field, grid northwest of the 1977 trench. While it is very similar to Paleo-Indian scrapers found elsewhere in the Eastern United States (Ritchie and Funk 1973:22, Plate 10), there were no diagnostic artifacts at the same level in the test pit.

This does raise the possibility that there is a second Paleo-Indian component occupation elsewhere in the same field. The reason that a second component is conjectured and not a continuation of the one being discussed is that this specimen stands out as being very different from the others. The flint is different in physical appearance. The workmanship is extensive on a very small piece of flint with extremely close retouching.

The only evidence for suggesting a temporal hiatus between the two occupations, if indeed this is Paleo-Indian, is entirely subjective. After two years of handling and examining the collection, this specimen has a very different, but vaguely familiar "feel". While tinged with elements of psychic archaeology, feelings such as these frequently lead to further, productive work. They also frequently lead to dead-ends. In this case the risk of weeks of fruitless searching for another Paleo-Indian component seems worth it. The worst possible outcome (not all that bad) would be more Archaic occupations.

Gravers (Plate 12, Table 11)

Gravers are differentiated from graving spurs and beaks by a purposefully made projection that shows extensive unifacial retouch on one lateral and occasionally unifacial retouch on the opposite face of the other lateral. Graving spurs (Plate 16) are intentionally flaked to isolate the spur, but the spur itself is not retouched. They appear to be less substantial than gravers, but usually have a strong medial ridge on their spurs for added strength. Beaks are more or less fortuitous. While used similarly to graving spurs they may or may not have been made intentionally. Striking platforms that are partially extant sometimes exhibit beaks when the edge of the bulb of percussion is damaged. They may occur fortuitously elsewhere on a flake simply by the intersection of two semicircular flakes leaving a small, pointed projection between them. Edge wear analysis should be used to distinguish between fortuitous (unused) and purposeful (utilized) beaks.

Of the five gravers two are multiple gravers, another two have definitely retouched areas not associated with the graving function, and the last is a fragment with a broken tip. Each will be described separately, and then the group will be described in general.

The spurred sidescraper (graver-sidescraper) (Plate 12a) was made on a flake with the remnants of a massive striking platform and a large, but not thick, bulb of percussion. The left lateral of the dorsal face was almost completely unifacially retouched, as was an unknown amount of the lower right lateral and distal end. The missing segment of the lower left lateral with its nearly right angle lateral fractures does not exhibit any of the patterns for lithic rejection illustrated by Callahan. It is probably due to a combination of factors with one cracking the stone and another creating a different fracture, as well as removing the segment along the fracture zone of the first flake. The missing segment of the lower right lateral near the distal end was caused by overshot. With the exception of the entire proximal end, the dorsal and ventral laterals of the missing segments, and the retouched edges, all ridges and edges are highly polished through use. The retouched edges would have lost their polish when resharpened or in further retouching for multi-functional tasks. The absence of polish on the laterals and ends mentioned could reflect the absence of polish through its period of usefulness or the breaks were due to reworking the flake for other functions. The second alternative is strongly suggested by the presence of a small scraper edge on the distal end between the two breaks. The breaks are definitely due to flaking problems and not material flaws, use breakage, dropping, etc., for the reasons cited previously.

The graver tip is an integral part of this implement and was not a result of secondary flaking on a spent scraper. The retouching on the scraping edge is very similar throughout and is differentially patinated or worn in the vicinity of the graver tip. The graver has a strategically placed medial ridge which extends to the tip for added strength. These traits are shown clearly in Plate 13.

The ventral face along the right lateral exhibits the removal of tiny flakes during utilization. A small negative bulb of percussion on the ventral face of the graver shows that the tip was broken away due to

61

pressure or impact from the dorsal side of the lateral. No attempt was made to retouch the graver after the break.

The other complete single graver with an additionally retouched area for a possible spokeshave function (Plate 12b) was placed at the distal end of a long flake. A portion of the original striking platform remains despite an attempt to remove it. that resulted in a shallow step fracture. The unifacial retouch on the distal end and left lateral of the dorsal face is fairly steep (55° to 65°) with a 75° angle on both sides of the graver tip. The only sign of wear is a minor tip break caused by pressure or a glancing blow from the right side directed toward the left. Although there is no wear evidenced on the ventral face, there is damage from the original flake detachment. Plate 14 clearly shows many similarities to Plate 13: retouching, isolation of tip, and medial ridge.

The fragmentary single graver (Plate 12c) has a broken tip with a retouched lateral on either side. Aside from edge polishing there is no other evidence of wear on the retouched ventral or dorsal laterals.

The first of the multiple gravers (Plate 12d) had at least three tips on the retouched distal end and adjacent left lateral of the dorsal face. The retouching utilization on the right lateral left a straight edge lacking in obviously retouched or obviously utilized characteristics. It seems to be both. Retouching on the striking platform removed a very large flake that straightened the edge. The ventral face clearly shows the bulb of percussion and edge-damaged laterals with no attempts to retouch and no consistent edge wear patterns.

The graver's tips were steeply retouched for strength. One is on a strong medial ridge, but the other two are not. One tip has been broken off nearly at the base, but on the other two polish is the only form of wear. On the whole, the great amount of wear on the specimen can be judged by the nearly vertical areas of retouch and utilization.

The other multiple graver (Plate 12e) is a double one on the distal end of a waste flake. The area adjacent to and between the tips is steeply retouched (75° to 80°) with the only evidence of wear being minute scars on the graver tips.

As is the case with the graving spurs, the similarities among these specimens are not in the overall morphology but in the manufacture and utilization of the projections. Gross size and thickness of the flake were not important, but how it was worked was. The graver tips are convex-plano, supported by strong medial ridges and steep retouch, and show edge wear. They were located at the distal (striking platform) end of the flake.

All of these traits were necessary for their function: piercing.

Graving spurs show consistent use for slitting, but gravers have a much stronger projection which pierced hides and possibly even bone and wood. The tip was located at the distal end of a flake to assure maximum strength. The medial ridge and steeply retouched sides added further strength and cutting edges. Heavy use would produce a lot of edge damage, polish on exposed medial ridges, as well as hand-held or hafted parts of the flake, and frequently broken tips. Tip symmetry was important for accurate piercing and an equal dispersion of the pressure. The convex-plano cross section of the tip assured efficient cutting edges, as well as a wedging effect as the graver was turned clockwise or counterclockwise into a material.

Having defined gravers from this collection according to the morphology of their working edges and the techniques for their manufacture, I cannot accept them as implements for engraving bone or eyeing bone needles. The working edges and edge wear are simply not consistent with these procedures. Previously published Paleo-Indian reports suggesting cutting functions of engraving and slitting needle eyes confused the distinctions between graving spurs and gravers as defined here.

Drill (Plate 12f, Table 11)

The distinction between a drill and a graver is a matter of length, overall size, and cross section of the tip. Although the tips have been broken from this drill, the remnants are significantly larger than the corresponding parts on the gravers. Gravers are flaked bilaterally and unifacially; and drills, bifacially, but not on a common lateral. The obverse of one tip was flaked on the left lateral; the reverse, on the right lateral. This gives the tip a biconvex cross section which differs from the convex-plano projection on gravers.

Functionally this makes a great deal of sense. A drill that is being pushed into a piece of wood or bone and turned simultaneously needs the edge sharpened by retouch to be supported from the other face. The edges of a bilaterally, bifacially flaked tip used in the same manner would be more susceptible to breaking since they would have very little support. This is the same reason that modern drill bits have a relatively narrow, steeply beveled cutting edge on a massive cylinder. The tip has to be sharpened for initial penetration, but the sharpened edges continue to cut as the drill twists deeper into the material being worked.

The single drill in this collection exhibits retouch and edge wear consisting of small-scale nibbling on the unflaked face of each lateral of the tip (Plate 15). This could only have occurred if the artifact was held between thumb and forefinger and turned counterclockwise. Since the edge wear is continuous to the base of the projection, the drill was being used for more than just piercing. Once it had penetrated, it was being twisted back and forth to enlarge the opening. This type of wear could have occurred in drilling relatively thin pieces where the width at the base of the tip was equal to the desired hole diameter, or pieces equal in thickness to the length of the original tip. The same tool could be for very different end products.

In the first instance the drill is used for reaming an opening to the desired diameter: perforating a flat bone pendant or ornament. The drill would have the advantage of leaving a clean, circular hole. In the second instance a circular hole is being bored into wood because no other tool can be used as effectively in making the hole. The clean, circular properties are not necessary, but a quickly made opening is. A related function suggested by the other two is as a ream to remove pith from a wooden shaft. The pith must be removed to a certain depth and leave a clean, circular hole of predictable diameter for inserting a projectile point or even a detachable foreshaft of a harpoon or barbed spear.

In the photograph (Plate 12f) the drill has an apparent endscraper between the broken tips. This is actually the fortuitous intersection of the lateral edges of the tips. This can be seen in a cross section view showing half of the edge beveled toward the dorsal and the other half beveled toward the ventral face. The absence of other retouch and edge wear reinforces the single-function nature of this tool. Although it may have been used to bore holes into both wood and bone for different reasons, it was not used as a scraper, knife, or anything other than a drill. It was a specialized implement.

The occurrence at this site of a variety of pointed implements (projectile point, graver, drill, and graving spur) does not imply that the projections were used in the same manner. A close analysis of the points shows many differences in their manufacture, physical appearance, and edge wear suggesting a variety of different functions. While it is true that the raw materials were limited to bone, stone, hides, wood and other plant products and that the materials being worked have a large role in determining edge wear, the nature of the tool's use, duration and intensity of use, and the motor habits of the user must be considered in interpreting the tool's function.

The only remaining question is whether this is actually Paleo-Indian. All of the quartz artifacts from the Paleo-Indian section of the site were found at the periphery of squares immediately adjacent to those having diagnostic flint artifacts or in levels immediately above those with diagnostic flint remains. Quartz debitage is found in very small quantity throughout the component, but no finished specimens are deep within it. No diagnostic Paleo-Indian artifacts were found in the same square as the drill. On the positive side are the manufacturing similarities to other definite Paleo-Indian artifacts and the gross dissimilarities to any of the Archaic material found at higher levels. While this cannot be positively assigned to the Paleo-Indian component, it is not out-of-place morphologically or functionally.

Graving Spurs (Plate 16, Table 12)

Graving spurs are unifacial implements serving various slitting functions. Because they were produced on waste flakes with a minimum of retouching, there is a wide variation in metrical attributes of length, width, thickness, and weight, as well as cross section, edge angles of the spur, and the location of the spur. The only trait exhibiting some consistency is the angle of utilized or retouched edges. Despite the numerous differences, this is a very homogeneous artifact category in terms of the manner of utilization as suggested by spur morphology and edge wear.

After selecting a convenient waste flake, the knapper isolated the spur by removing usually two flakes from the dorsal face. Although minor retouch may be present elsewhere on the flake, the spur is never retouched. Its sharpness results from the initial flake removal. To support this sharp, thin projection during use, a medial ridge extends from the central part of the flake to the tip of the spur.

Edge wear analysis of each entire graving spur revealed other consistencies. Most of the spurs showed evidence of utilization in the form of nibbling, tip fracture, polish, or combinations of these ranging from very minor to severe. Although the spur and immediately adjacent laterals were most frequently the site of wear, other parts of some also exhibited wear. In the few instances of ventral edge wear, its length, width, and intensity is markedly less than with dorsal wear. Deliberate flaking and edge wear are clearly shown in Plate 17.

Since nibbling on the spur or the area immediately adjacent to it is the most prevalent type of edge wear, the action producing this wear must be occurring most of the time the graving spur is in use. Nibbling is a very gradual process resulting from pressure of the implement against the material being worked. Dorsal nibbling occurs when the dorsal face is up and pressure is exerted downward.

Polish is also a very slow process caused by the constant rubbing of the tool against a fine-grained material. The finer the grain of the material being worked, the finer the polish. The polished surfaces in this sample show no sign of individual striations at even

40X magnification.

The most traumatic type of edge wear present on the graving spurs is impact fracture. This results from a sudden impact of a hard material against the edge or tip of the spur. All of the broken spur tips show a narrow flake scar running from the extant portion of the spur along the medial ridge. The scar is longer than one would expect from the thin tip being snapped by heavy pressure. The impact fracture on the side of a spur was a pair of negative bulbs of percussion.

The location of these three types of edge wear is a further clue to the manner in which the tool was used. Since most of the edge wear is on the dorsal face adjacent to the more acute edge of the spur and the spur is usually located on the lateral rather than an end, the tip does not bear the brunt of the pressure during use. The tip's function is to pierce the soft material enough to get the more acute edge of the spur in position for slicing. The acute edge and tip are supported not only by the medial ridge but also by the less acute trailing edge. The less intensive and less frequent wear evidence of the trailing edge suggests a slitting motion in one direction occurs most, but not all, of the time.

Depending upon the width of the material being slit or the angle at which the graving spur is being held, the length of nibbling or polish will vary. Another variable is the duration of the task. Polish will not develop as rapidly as nibbling under any circumstances, but neither will occur if the task is of very short duration.

These conclusions concerning the function of graving spurs also apply to those specimens not having edge wear or tip damage (Table 12). Since the degree of cumulative, as opposed to traumatic, edge wear is relative to the duration of the task(s) performed, it is possible that artifacts manufactured in the same way as graving spurs were actually used for a very short period of time. Some of the graving spurs outlived their period of usefulness and were discarded without edge wear. Since these are rapidly made on available waste flakes, they are easy to pick up, chip, use, and discard. This could account for graving spurs lacking prominent medial ridges, as well as edge wear. If they broke during use, they could be rapidly replaced.

The slicing or slitting functions assigned to these tools encompasses a wide variety of materials that could have been worked. Possible uses are slitting of reeds for baskets; of stalks for food; of hides for rawhide strips; of bone splinters for eyed needles; and of wood or bone for decoration. Wood, bone, and hides are more likely to produce polish or nibbling on tools than reeds or stalks. Wood and bone are more likely to break the tip off of a spur than hides, reeds, or stalks. The problem is not to find the single material which will cause all of the different types of edge wear seen but to prove either that these tools were not used for each of these functions at different times or that some were used for one function and others for the remaining functions.

This analysis has shown the nature of the similarities among the graving spurs: They were made unifacially on waste flakes. Edge wear is usually nibbling on the more acute side of the spur. Tip damage is relatively minor. Most of the edge wear is associated with the spur and not other parts of the flake. Although the range of possible materials being worked includes bone, hide, wood, and plant stalks, the type of work is primarily slitting with the side of the spur rather than piercing with the tip.

This important distinction serves to functionally differentiate graving spurs from gravers. Graver tips are purposely retouched for piercing. More importantly the presence of retouched areas (scrapers?) on gravers not associated with the tips suggests a dual purpose related to fulfilling a single task. Although graving spurs do occasionally have utilized/retouched sections not associated with the spur, these are not numerous.

Knives (Plate 18, Table 13)

Knives are differentiated from scrapers and other edged implements (as opposed to pointed ones) on the basis of their nearly symmetrical biconvex edge profiles. Neither of the knives in this collection has been retouched to make the symmetrical edge. The edge was produced by the removal of a very large flake on either face. Utilization also differs from that on other edged implements in that it is bifacial on a common edge. This type of wear is expected on specimens which have a sharp, biconvex edge lacking support on the trailing face or edge.

The first knife (Plate 18a) has a far sharper edge than the other one but with a similar array of bifacial impact fractures and nibbling. Slight polish in the form of edge rounding on the impact scars is also present.

The edge angles of the second specimen (Plate 18b) are not as acute as the first, making its knife function less plausible. This is a large cortical flake which was struck from a core with a hard hammer causing a huge bulb of percussion and minor stress cracks. Utilization is evident on the ventral right lateral and dorsal left lateral. Impact fractures with small, but obvious negative bulbs of percussion interspersed with sporadic nibbling on the ventral face contrasts with the more closely spaced nibbling separated from the numerous impact fractures on the dorsal face of the same lateral (Plate 18b).

67

Minor polishing up to 1.5mm wide on the lower right ventral extends to the distal end.

I am not entirely pleased with the "knife" classification of this artifact. The bifacial edge symmetry, edge angles at the upper range for knives, and edge damage which is similar to that of a more subjectively believable knife are important morphological traits. But the absence of a really sharp section on the working edge and the evidence that such an edge was never extant are very strong considerations to suggest alternative functions.

The biconvex edge cross section could have been used as an excellent heavy duty wedge. Battering on adjacent sides and on the cortex could have been by repeated blows from a wooden billet. Because of the minor nature of the impact fractures and the absence of retouching on the working edge, bone or dry, soft wood splitting could have been done. Both will yield readily to a dull blade wedging the sides apart.

The possible use as a chopper is not plausible even though it does bear a physical resemblance to one. The edge damage is not sufficiently severe for a tool which was cracking green bones or severing joints.

Spokeshave (Plate 19, Table 13)

The functional term "spokeshave" is used because of the morphology of the working edge: a semi-circular notch with retouching and/or utilization. This is contradicted by edge damage, the narrowness of the notch, and many similarities to graving spurs. The fortuitous resemblance to a spokeshave is a result of a series of accidental fractures and utilization of a purposely flaked tool.

A pair of very deep negative bulbs of percussion isolated three massive projections. One of these was snapped off leaving a very jagged stump with a partial step fracture, "chatter" (sharply peaked ripple marks), and a hinge fracture on the reverse. Because a simple step fracture resulting from overshot or material flaw would have left a neat, clean stump, this fracture resulted from too much pressure against a hard material or a direct blow. The central projection was also snapped off during use. The third projection has only minor tip damage.

The third projection resembles a very massive graving spur with its single, utilized/retouched lateral, sharp tip, supporting trailing edge, and medial ridge. Because of the proximity of the central projection, the third tip could have been used only for working materials thin enough to fit between them.

The edge wear between the two projections was caused by severe pressure being applied against the ventral face. The most obvious edge wear on the ventral face is the wide, deep flake scars having nearly vertical nibbling. Were this caused by slitting, the material being slit would have been drawn toward the notch between the projections and most of the edge wear would have been evidenced there. This is not the case. Most severe edge wear is present on the portion of the lateral nearer the tip, suggesting that slitting or splitting functions were not being done.

An activity which fits all of the evidence (steep nibbling, sharp tip, sharp lateral, and supporting edge in a narrow notch) is the scraping of thin, hard materials such as bone or wood. The sharp tip is used in gouging out imperfections or in shallow cutting to loosen material to be removed by further scraping.

This is a function similar to that of a spokeshave in that a hard material is being scraped smooth. It is different because spokeshaves removed the material to leave a smooth cylinder, and this tool was making a smooth, flat surface.

Retouched Flakes (Plate 20, Table 14)

This category is not a true artifact type because of the absence of shared morphological traits, as well as criteria for determining their (intended) function. Retouched flakes are differentiated from utilized flakes by the fact that, although utilization may have occurred, there are no wear marks. Although other artifacts from this collection were retouched, this category is limited to tools not fitting the other artifact types.

The striking platform on the flake (Plate 20a) was retouched subsequent to the severe step fracture on the dorsal face. The retouching may have been done to make a beak on the right side of the proximal end, which would have been strengthened during use by the massive striking platform and its bulb of percussion. The problem with the beak being made intentionally for use is that the right lateral is far too thin to support the perforating or slicing functions ascribed to beaks. Scars from a lateral snap near the beak could evidence a broken graving spur with subsequent rejuvenation of the flake and a change in its function. However, conjecture of this nature is analogous to spelunkers discussing the number of miles unexplored, unmapped passages in Mammoth Cave.

The second specimen (Plate 20b) has been retouched on the ventral face of the striking platform and on the dorsal right lateral. The lateral retouch is suggestive of an endscraper, but the specimen is far too thin to support a scraping edge with an angle of less than 30 degrees. This acute angle is more typically associated with knives, but the large flake scars are not.

A retouched quartz flake (Plate 20c) has no apparent function. The possibility does exist that this was rejected because of material flaws. Material flaw is discernible on the flat surface of the dorsal face where a contact zone between this piece and another material or other quartz intrusion occurred. It is a naturally weak area susceptible to being sheared off by percussion rather than being flaked. While it is likely that it is part of a larger piece being retouched, this cannot be said with certainty. There are too few quartz specimens from the site to determine if this material was worked in the same way as flint. The lack of homogeneity in the locally available quartz makes it very difficult to work.

The last (Plate 20d) was probably a portion of a bifacial reject being worked into a tool. The retouched hook or beak was probably never used since the thin edges of the immediately adjacent lateral are still sharp. Had the beak been utilized, these edges would have been crushed, nicked, or otherwise broken or damaged. The deliberate nature of the retouching to form the beak is suggested because this shape is not seen in any of the other rejected or unfinished bifaces.

Hammerstone (Plate 21, Table 15)

The quartz hammerstone was rather high in the stratigraphic profile to be definitely Paleo-Indian but a little deep for the Archaic components. It is included here for consideration since core reduction was occurring, albeit minimally, as evidenced by the few cortical flakes and cores with cortex. One would not expect a large number of hammerstones for lithic reduction. While a few pits are present, the evidence is far from conclusive that it was used solely for lithic reduction. It is possible, however, that this implement served one or more of the functions of hammerstones: bone breaking, plant crushing, or nut cracking.

Debitage

The careful analysis of debitage, chips, waste flakes, detritus, or lithic debris has been an oft neglected source of valuable insights into the lifeways of a site's previous occupants. Until very recently the finished artifacts were the primary or even sole data discussed in a site report. The debitage was reported by count, weight, and lithic type, but was not usually discussed in detail. While this study did not exhaust all of the possible avenues of analysis, many interesting insights were obtained.

The debitage from the Paleo-Indian component consisted of 7229 flint and 131 quartz pieces ranging in weight from .1gm to 8.4gm. Although none of the quartz pieces were cortical, bifacial thinning flakes, or heat damaged, these attributes did occur in the flint group. Each of these will be considered separately and in association with unfinished and completed artifacts.

All of the 12 cortical flint flakes were small, smooth, and water-polished, suggesting that the original cobble(s) from which they came was not very large or at least did not have very much cortex removed. The presence of two finished artifacts (Plates 11c, 18b) exhibiting cortex demonstrates that complete decortication was not a prerequisite to utilization. Cortical flakes also prove that flint cobbles from the Shepaug River adjacent to the site were one source of lithic material. A search of the river banks within 20m of the site yielded small flint cobbles of the same color and texture as the flint flakes from the Paleo-Indian component.

The quantity of cortical flakes compared to the total number of waste flakes can be interpreted in two ways. Decortication was not a frequent activity here because a few large cobbles could have provided all of the flint needed to account for the discarded implements and the waste flakes, or decortication was not a necessary manufacturing step since flint cobbles provided only some of the raw material. The rejuvenation of previously made tools and the working of chunks or blanks decorticated elsewhere might have been the source of most of the debitage. The best way to resolve this dilemma is to reconstruct the original cobbles from cores, chunks, blanks, artifacts and the 7229 flint chips.

Although bifacial thinning flakes (Plate 22, Table 15) were removed in the process of manufacturing bifaces, not all 253 are only waste flakes. Some were either utilized or retouched for use (Plate 10l). These flakes were produced during the lateral or, more rarely, end thinning of bifaces. The long, flat striking platform was prepared on a dorsal lateral by transverse flaking and abrasion. A wooden or antler billet was used to strike the prepared platform causing a long, thin flake to "peel off" of the ventral face. After a series of these had been driven from the ventral face, the biface was turned over and a series was driven from the dorsal face. The continued removal of bifacial thinning flakes gradually reduced the thickness of the biface. Very careful control was required lest too much of the lateral be removed, too thick a flake be removed causing a fracture, or too long a flake be removed causing an overshot. All of these

71

could be a reason for rejecting the biface.

Because of these stringent functional requirements, the morphological similarity among bifacial thinning flakes at a single site and among closely related sites is expected to be very high and the acceptable range of idiosyncratic variation low. The present collection exhibits a very narrow range of variation. Figs. 12, 13 show that the frequency distribution of bifacial thinning flakes by weight and striking platform angles are tightly clustered.

About 75% of the specimens exhibit a striking platform prepared by a combination of abrasion and transverse flaking. They are easily differentiated from ordinary waste flakes not only by the diagnostic large platform angle, but also by the large, flat platform being at least one-quarter as long as the remainder of the flake is wide. Variations from these generalizations require some explanation.

A total of only 17% of the bifacial thinning flakes have extant transverse flake scars on the edge of the striking platform nearest the ventral face. Because a portion of the striking platform in this vicinity was usually crushed or subsequently flaked, it is possible that evidence of abrasion had been removed. In the 4% of the cases where abrasion was the sole means for preparing the striking platform, it was severe to the point of nearly being polish. These platforms differed from the normal long and flat by being narrower, peaked, and having a generally smaller platform angle. The remaining striking platforms were flaked laterally or in combination with abrading and transverse flaking.

It is apparent that a strong, long striking platform was necessary for successful bifacial thinning. Although abrasion was usually used to achieve the proper striking surface, transverse and lateral flaking alone did not occasionally produce a suitable platform.

The use of a wooden or antler billet is inferred for many reasons. This is a very controllable percussion instrument not only because the end can be fashioned or re-fashioned to the proper angle, but also because the knapper has a good handle with which to direct his blows. The minimal platform damage shows that the flake was removed with an instrument having some "give" which allowed the shock of impact to be dissipated gradually. Had a hard hammer (stone) been used, crushing, a prominent bulb of percussion, ripple marks, or even stress cracks would be more commonly found on these flakes. They occurred very rarely and in only a minor way.

The heat damaged flakes consist of 32 specimens. Most of the heat damage was potlidding, but some color changes were also attributed to heating. There are too few specimens to determine if the heating was actually a step in the manufacturing process or simply waste flakes being discarded into a hearth. The absence of hearths at the site could be seen as evidence of purposeful heat treating at another location to make the stone more workable. The problem with this notion, in addition to the lack of agreement among modern knappers as to the efficacy of such treatment, is that the heat damaged specimens are not consistent. Some are cortical, others are bifacial thinning or retouch flakes. The debate will not be solved in this study.

The association of bifacial thinning flakes with finished artifacts and debitage is very strong. Fig. 8 shows the distribution of these flakes and debitage within each square and each level. A comparison of this to Fig. 10 showing the distribution of finished artifacts by level, by square, by type demonstrates only part of this association. Since the 1.5m square is an archaeological construct and not part of the original inhabitants' lifeway, it should not be used as the sole means for interpreting the data. The same is true, but to a lesser degree, of the 5cm arbitrary levels. A chart showing the distribution of artifacts according to levels can be made to very closely approximate the actual depth of the artifacts below datum. Clusters will still stand out. Admittedly this is second best to using precise depth, but since all of that information was not available with the excavation plan used, this will suffice.

Removing the artificial barriers of the squares and combining all of the relevant data into a single chart showing the levels across the entire site, does not create theoretical problems of over-simplification. Since the hypothesis is that the site is the result of a single occupation over a short period of time, all of the squares were occupied contemporaneously and can therefore be combined. When combined in this way, it is obvious from Fig. 10 that the levels having bifacial thinning flakes are more likely to have flint artifacts than those levels lacking bifacial flakes. I don't think this is some magnetic attraction, but that the bifacial thinning flakes were being produced on the spot in the process of manufacturing the artifacts recovered. The artifact analysis bears this out in two ways: the bifacial flakes are from flint having the same physical traits as the artifacts, and the other chippage includes trimming and retouching flakes.

Not all of the bifacial flakes were discarded. Many of the finished artifacts have remnants of the same type of striking platform, platform angle, and plano cross sectional traits.

Another category of chippage is the channel flake. While it has been included here under the artifact category, it is actually only a by-product of manufacture that was seldom used. Channel flakes are actually medial thinning flakes. Most of the bifacial removal has occurred along the laterals of the artifacts prior to the removal or attempted removal of the medial flakes. The numerous scars on the dorsal face of these specimens attest to the regular nature of the removal of relatively wide flakes. A medial ridge is very common and must be removed prior to the use of the biface.

The remainder of the flint flakes and the quartz flakes from the Paleo-Indian component range in size from primary decortication chunks to retouching flakes. Although no concerted effort was made to fit broken flakes together from different levels and/or squares, several fits were found in the course of analysis.

The last phase of the analysis was to bring all of the data together into meaningful tables, figures, and plates which would accurately present them, as well as show meaningful associations. Some of the associations immediately obvious in the depictions would not have been noticed had these depictions not been done.

This is where the interaction among excavation, analysis and interpretation is seen most clearly and, potentially, could lead to misinterpretations based upon accidental associations. Using Fig. 10 as an example, what would have been the impact of 1m squares and 30cm levels on that distribution of artifacts? This cannot be answered because the excavation units cannot be restructured into smaller units. If the distribution of artifacts were different, would this have changed the interpretation slightly, moderately, totally, or not at all? If the excavation units had changed in size, would the cluster of flint chips still be associated with the bifacial thinning flakes and the discarded artifacts?

Future researchers will have to examine those questions with different excavation plans. However, current researchers will be able to examine the present interpretations on the basis of the data presented here.

CHAPTER THREE

When this book was in the planning stages, my intention was to present a detail comparison of 6LF21 to published data from other Paleo-Indian sites in the Northeast in particular and in the Eastern United States in general. This proved to be extremely difficult to accomplish in detail and only slightly less difficult in general. As a criticism of the end-product and not of the individuals responsible, publications seldom include the basic observations of weight, length, width, thickness; associations by excavation unit of square and level; detailed counts or weights of chippage by excavation unit; individual descriptions of artifacts; and photographs of all specimens. While a reasonable case can be made for summarizing collections having hundreds of specimens, comparisons are very difficult to make.

Comparisons not only are difficult to make, but data for a different or more intensive interpretation are also lacking. Since this is not one of those ubiquitous "Preliminary Reports" which is never followed by a more intensive analysis, the possibility that someone will utilize my data to "scoop" me on a site I excavated is not of concern. Publishing my observations on all of the excavated specimens using a selection from all of the possible array of analytical techniques and measurements is an open invitation for anyone to use it. If George MacDonald, Leonard Eisenberg, or Herbert Kraft wish to re-examine the distribution or functions of artifacts from Debert, Twin Fields, or Plenge in light of my interpretations, they will have the raw data from which those interpretations were drawn.

I don't mean to personally criticize anyone for not publishing raw data for any reason (no time for a detailed analysis of 5,000 specimens, publisher wouldn't devote 35 pages to charts, or future plans for more analysis after publishing a preliminary report), but this practice would facilitate comparison and could be the only record the world will ever have of the data.

A close reading of *The Bull Brook Site in Relation to "Fluted*

Point" Manifestations in Eastern North America (Jordan 1960) shows that all of the specimens were uncataloged and kept in private homes when he began the study. The same was true of the material from Plenge [Fig. 1 (9)] surface collected prior to Kraft's excavation. When the original specimens are dispersed and uncataloged among a large number of collectors, the potential for loss due to natural disaster, theft, and post-mortem distribution is greatly enhanced. If anything were to happen to the original specimens, the only record would be the notes of the analyst. Unless these are published or multiple copies distributed to safe repositories, the risk of total loss is extremely high. I hope that this situation is not exacerbated by an "If-I-can't-publish-it, no-one-will" attitude.

The nature of the comparisons will be much more general than intended except in instances where a certain type of data was published. The Paleo-Indian tool kit is functionally similar from site to site. Hunting, butchering, hideworking, bone working, woodworking, and manufacturing are evidenced by projectile points, knives, scrapers, gravers, spokeshaves, and debitage. The use of unifacial implements usually far exceeds the bifacial ones. Flint (chert), jasper, and, to a lesser degree, quartz are preferred lithics.

This generalization concerning function and lithic preference exhibits a great deal of stylistic variation from site to site. The occurrence of miniature points, "pumpkin seed" points (Kraft 1973:77), bifacially-flaked gravers, and the usual extremes in sizes of other artifacts may be more a temporal phenomenon than a functional or stylistic one.

Seldom seen artifacts, decorative/magical/ceremonial ones and pièces esquillées (wedge for bone or wood splitting), make one site stand out in the minds of researchers, but the reasons for the paucity of certain artifacts cannot be known. Pièces esquillées might be present at more sites than Debert and Plenge but were not recognized as an expended tool. The near absence of carved or engraved artifacts from Paleo-Indian sites does not necessarily suggest a dearth of the aesthetic. Their primary artistic expression could have been in media other than those preserved or maybe we are unable to recognize the aesthetic senses of people living 10,000 years ago.

The duration or size of an occupation is a frequently debated point in site reports. The concept of a small, mobile band occupying a site for a very short period of time, whether it is a few weeks or a few months, recurs repeatedly despite the amount of debitage and the frequencies of different artifacts. If the count is low, the band is smaller and the stay shorter or less intensive than if the count were higher. When a point is reached that the band is no longer small and the stay subjectively approaches a year, then the site was re-occupied repeatedly according to the hypothesis of the researcher.

While this is a generalization doing an injustice to the exceptions, the point is that the criteria for determining size of band and duration of occupation are subjectively interpreted because the objective data are absent. The primary problem is the remarkable amount of disturbance at the majority of Paleo-Indian sites due to natural and modern cultural causes. Even though the concentration of artifacts may give the impression that the site does bear a resemblance to its former self at the time of abandonment, the amount of horizontal and vertical migration of artifacts could be significant. An example of this is cited by Jordan (1960:193). Fitting pieces of a fluted point found *"only"* (emphasis mine) 99 feet apart in two different "hot spots" suggested the simultaneous occupation of a relatively large area. Since only "hot spots" were dug by the excavators and not the area between these artifact concentrations, the likelihood is that massive horizontal displacement occurred moving one fragment away from the other. Had this actually been a series of single occupations, the artifact concentrations should have been more continuously distributed. Whether or not the expected actually occurred cannot be tested in the field since the site has been destroyed.

A second reason for suggesting a multiple occupation or a disturbinary context is an extraordinary quantity of any particular artifact. A case in point is Debert where MacDonald reported 362 endscrapers from a single excavation area which he believed corresponded to a single camp. I cannot imagine how many people it would take to make, utilize, and discard 362 endscrapers at a single camp over an indeterminate number of days, weeks, or months. This must have been an incredibly intensive and specialized occupation to use that many endscrapers and still fit the model of a small, mobile band in a seasonal round.

It is an unfortunate reality, but I have yet to see all of the data necessary for comparisons being published in a site report. There are always unanswered questions and measurements or observations which were not made. This is simply because no one can second-guess the future. Observations which are obvious to one researcher will never occur to another because the need never arose. The best one can hope for is that enough data are presented, which will illustrate the nature of the artifacts well enough that a future researcher will know that certain observations are possible if only he were to study the collection for himself. For this reason all of the artifacts from the site are pictured and the debitage has been generally summarized.

This work has not been as comparative as it could have been to other Paleo-Indian collections from the Northeast. Part of this is due to time constraints which preclude the same intensive analysis of the much larger collections extant from Bull Brook [Fig. 1 (3)], Debert, Plenge, and others. A comparative study of that nature prior to the publication of the initial site report would have taken years. The initial site report has taken two years and should be presented for outside review prior to a comparative study.

THEORETICAL CONSIDERATIONS

One of the most important considerations in the study of Paleo-Indian is one of change. What changes occurred during the Paleo-Indian stage prior to the advent of the Early Archaic technical changes? This problem is approachable only from the excavation of stratified, single component sites. William Gardner and Robert Verrey review previous efforts at establishing a chronology for Paleo-Indian and suggest that length-width ratios of fluted points would be useful in creating a tripartite division: Clovis, Middle Paleo, and Dalton-Hardaway (1979:13-46). While they do show that their method works for a small sample from sealed stratified components at the Thunderbird and Fifty Sites of the Flint Run Complex [Fig. 1 (13)], an attempt to apply it to Shoop [Fig. 1 (11)] and Williamson [Fig. 1 (14)] site data is flawed. The flaw is not that Williamson shows both Clovis and Middle Paleo and that Shoop shows only Clovis Sub-Phase, but that they attempted to test their hypotheses on non-stratified, probably multiple occupation, surface sites.

"As previously indicated, little typological evidence exists for temporal change resulting in stages of development within the Northeastern Paleo-Indian assemblages characterized by Clovis or similar projectile points" (Funk 1976:228). The reason for this is painfully obvious. Given all of the excavated Paleo-Indian sites for which a detailed report has been published (Debert, Bull Brook, Shoop, Reagan [Fig. 1 (2)], West Athens Hill [Fig. 1 (5)], Kings Road [Fig. 1 (4)], Williamson), the absence of sealed, stratified, single component occupations precludes typological evidence useful for studying temporal changes. There are too many other factors which are obscuring the picture of a site at a single point in time.

Repeated occupations over a few hundred years would have introduced changes due to advances in tool technology, differences in site function, differences in tool use, personal variation in manufacturing or use, and admixture with previous and subsequent artifacts. It is impossible to study change without isolating a series of

78

points in time. Once a series of single component, undisturbed Paleo-Indian sites are available for detailed analysis, then variation can be studied. If the sites are very close to one another, then the effects of spatial separation can be minimized as a variable. If the sites functioned similarly and/or were occupied at the same season, suggesting a similar range of functions, the effect of another variable can be minimized. There are many variables to consider when studying the differences between sites or when attempting to better understand the sequence in the development and eventual evolution of Paleo-Indian technology, lifestyles, and culture.

It is impossible to construct *ex post facto* typologies on mixed components to compare them to other mixed components to better understand how culture differs from site to site or time to time. A mixed component site reveals a mosaic view caused by the overlaying of functionally different and temporally different occupations. Any attempt to sort them would be to impose 20th-century preconceptions of what "should" be together in a 10,000-year-old culture. The only way to see what that culture was like is to excavate sealed, single component sites.

A second problem in constructing typologies based only on projectile points is that there are so many other equally important variables that are being ignored. Tool manufacturing techniques, other categories of artifacts, and exploitive strategies are also subject to change through time. Cultures are well integrated wholes which could not and cannot function as discrete parts. To study only one aspect of a culture to understand the sequence of its development is to deny all of current anthropological theory. Consider the plight of the archaeologist of the 25th century who decides that Coke bottles are diagnostic artifacts worthy of a typological study. He will have to assume that it was one big, happy, cohesive world with everyone participating in the same activity. His analysis will show great similarities at a single point in time, but he is missing out on the vast technological, sociological, and ideological differences inherent in life as we know it around the world today.

Another recent approach to compare Paleo-Indian sites typologically is fallaciously based, biased, and a hopeless theoretical *cul-de-sac*. Leonard Eisenberg sought to compare unifacially worked artifacts from Plenge, West Athens Hill, Kings Road, Port Mobil [Fig. 1 (10)], Shawnee-Minisink, and Twin Fields using a cluster analysis. His first problem was in randomly selecting his sample to analyze for each collection. He used 14%, 30%, 60% from each of the first three sites and 100% of the available artifacts from the other three. The implicit assumption in random sampling is that the sample which is analyzed is representative of the entire collection. Since his selection was not based upon a weighted sampling from each functional class of tools, but rather upon a percentage from each provenience unit at non-stratified (with Shawnee-Minisink being an exception), potentially multi-component sites, the sample cannot be typical of the collection and any results will have an unpredictable bearing upon reality.

Assuming that the sample selected was sufficiently large to mitigate the effects of the selection technique, further flaws are still present. Rather than segregate each collection by the tool types or functions suggested, Eisenberg groups all of the variables for describing all types of tools into a single statistical formula to determine a coefficient of similarity for all of the tools. The use of a total of 52 qualitative and quantitative variables to reduce each tool to a single number supposedly facilitates comparison by removing the bias of the human observer. Two numbers which are (nearly) identical are supposedly a more accurate gauge of the similarity of two tools than the human eye and mind.

Since all 52 variables will not apply to a single specimen, a large number will never be used in a given comparison. If 26 apply to one specimen and the other 26 apply to a second specimen, it is theoretically possible to obtain identical numbers which will apply to very different specimens. While this is not likely, it is more likely that diagnostic traits designating very different functions will have so little weight in the statistical analysis that two tools will appear to be similar numerically but are actually functionally discrete. There can be no substitute for the initial morphological functional analysis to ensure that truly comparable items are being compared.

The numerical coefficients of similarity were clustered by use of a dendrogram which linked the clusters having similar values into major groupings. Although he summarizes each of the clusters and the major groupings for each site, Eisenberg does not present any raw data in the form of measurements, counts, weights, or even photographs for the reader to judge the efficacy of the statistical work. When discussing the Twin Fields Site in detail in the Appendix, he never reinforces the statistical conclusions with other data or assigns cluster designations to any of the artifact photographs.

The ultimate abuse of statistics occurs when he gives percentages and means for measurements taken on two artifacts (p. 91, Table X). With a sample of two the mean is either identical to the value of both specimens or it has no meaning. Since the mean is supposed to facilitate the description of the distribution of a particular measurement, it has no meaning whatsoever with two different measurements. The mean will be precisely halfway between them and typical of neither. Percentages are only meaningful with a sample that approaches or exceeds 50. With very small samples generalizations are nearly meaningless since the addition of a few new specimens will change the percentages several points. With large samples the addition of a few new specimens will have much less of a relative impact. Percentages on a sample of two are ridiculous. Fifty percent is only one. Add another specimen and the percentage drops to 33%. With a small sample a table of actual measurements is the most meaningful and least deceptive.

Eisenberg's stated goal of using cluster analysis as a means of finding "certain recurrent combinations of attribute values and to judge those artifacts expressing these combinations as constituting a distinct class or category" (1978:49) is not farfetched or unrealistic, but his approach was both. Cluster analysis is not some all encompassing panacea that will compensate for mixed components and the lack of a carefully detailed corpus of data. A better use of cluster analysis would have been to study each separate class of similarly appearing artifacts to ascertain whether they were merely morphologically similar or actually functionally similar despite morphological dissimilarities. A sample of a dozen could have been done simply by the researcher knowing each piece and remembering important traits. However, the real utility of cluster analysis is to be able to take thousands of specimens which have already been individually described and to compare them. The human mind cannot tackle this task as quickly and accurately as the computerized cluster analysis.

Cluster analysis, like any statistical technique, is merely a descriptive aid in the pursuit of an interpretative end (Hodson 1971). It is only a means and not an end in itself. If the computerized techniques deny reality by giving results which are unusable or do not fit the other facts, it is only the fault of the researcher. Computers and statistics are only tools to assist the researcher. If the researcher is guided by faulty theories or confused data, so is the computer: GIGO, Garbage In, Garbage Out. The true test of any analysis, whether it is statistical or not, is whether or not it yields usable information.

I do not foresee theoretical problems precluding a typological separation of the Paleo-Indian stage into a series of temporally discrete subunits. Carbon-14 dating is not capable of differentiating sites with sufficient precision, but by identifying diagnostic traits of early and late Paleo-Indian, the middle will fall into place. This will not happen by analyzing a single trait through time, nor will it come as a result of "super-sophisticated" number-crunching from surface, multi-component, functionally discrete, and/or disturbed sites. The key is in the exhaustive analysis and comparison of undisturbed, short-term, single occupation sites. It is impossible to define a point in time if one does not even know the characteristics of that point in time. Once the basic chronology has been established for a diversity of typological traits, then the work can begin segregating the mixtures from Bull Brook, Debert (?), Williamson, etc.

There is a larger problem in the theoretical concepts surrounding Paleo-Indian. On a macroscale there is remarkable homogeneity exhibited among all Paleo-Indian sites. The presence of fluted points, gravers, end/sidescrapers; the preponderance of unifacial tools; a date about 10,000 years ago; big-game hunting and/or processing are common. While there are also differences between sites, the number of similarities suggests something is wrong.

Archaeologists have defined Paleo-Indian so precisely based upon its previous occurrences in the Western United States that the true diversity of the culture may be overlooked. Since a real Paleo-Indian site has to include at least one fluted point, it is not at all strange to see an emphasis upon hunting, butchering, and animal processing for all Paleo-Indian sites. But this was only one aspect of their lives. Since it is now known that Paleo-Indians ate fish and had access to red oak, where are their fishing camps and acorn processing stations? These are seen for other cultures, why not Paleo-Indians?

Until tools for these tasks have been recognized in a Paleo-Indian context having fluted points, they can never be recognized outside that context. The same is true of sites predating the earliest fluted points in a given area. Are they actually Paleo-Indian sites which were not big game-hunting oriented? A case in point is Meadowcroft Rockshelter [Fig. 1 (12)] which has a series of C-14 dates in a stratified context spanning nearly 18,000 years (Adovasio, *et al.* 1977). Technically it does not have a Paleo-Indian component because it lacks fluted points. It could very well have been occupied by the same people who were called Paleo-Indians when they left a fluted point behind on the surface a few miles away.

The answer is not to call everything Paleo-Indian just because it has the appropriate age. This would deny the utility of classifications which are meant to be shorthand labels. It is very convenient that there are so many similarities covered by the term Paleo-Indian. This saves a lot of needless explanation every time the term is used. If it is to continue to be useful, the precision has to be maintained. Be aware of the potential limitations of using a term which applies to only a fragment of a culture. When it can be shown that a site lacking fluted points is actually a functioning part of the culture which made fluted points, then it should be included in the definition. There is the possibility that two or more different cultural adaptations are co-existing, each with its own diagnostic artifacts. In this case lumping them into a single category would only confuse the picture of what life was like 10,000 years ago.

Traditionally the interpretation of an occupation area as being a base, hunting, butchering, quarry, or whatever kind of camp was dependent upon the variety of implements recovered and their supposed functions. A hunting camp should have implements associated with preparations for the hunt. A butchering camp would have a different array of tools as would each of the other types of camps. The base camp should evidence the greatest variety of tools because more functions are being served, and the implicit assumption is that the variety of tools for a variety of functions also has a bearing upon the duration of that camp's occupation. A group of people staying for several months should do everything necessary for survival, thus leaving the greatest array of different specimens. Because their lifestyle could not support full-time specialists, the specialized activity had to be very short-term and their tool array would have been smaller.

The traditional assumptions have an inherent problem. They do not seem to hold true at 6LF21. A very small site with a mass of manufacturing debris concentrated with the expended implements exhibits a great diversity of activities, suggesting a base camp, but the temporal implications are that this camp was occupied for a very, very short term (a week? month?).

The quantity of debitage if taken alone would suggest a workshop area. The artifacts taken alone would suggest a base camp because of the diversity of functionally different tasks suggested. Put both of them together with the small area occupied and it makes a very short-term camp with basic manufacturing, reworking, sharpening; utilization of the completed or reworked tools; the discarding of worn-out tools; and the manufacture of tools for future use. The future-use interpretation comes from the large quantity of channel flakes and the presence of only a single, broken fluted point. Since this point was broken during manufacture, possibly another was subsequently made for future use. The next camp the occupants of 6LF21 made could be in the same field, in the same valley, or in an adjacent valley or state. But this camp was abandoned after a relatively short stay.

Duration of occupation is not a function of a type of camp being occupied, nor is the camp type a marker for duration. Butchering camps re-occupied during successive hunts may appear to be single long-term occupations. Short-term processing camps (butchering, hide working and bone working of the same carcasses; with a few people processing plants, preparing wooden shafts; and making the necessary implements for all of these) can appear to be long-term base camps because of the great variety of functionally different tools recovered in a small area. Had there been no indication that most of this site had been excavated, this could have been interpreted as a small sample from a much larger base camp. The clues for camp function and duration of occupation must be evaluated separately, as well as jointly.

CHAPTER FOUR

6LF21 is the oldest carbon-14 dated site in Connecticut and the only one in the state known to have an undisturbed Paleo-Indian component. The other Paleo-Indian sites in the state are surface find spots, disturbed contexts having an admixture of another culture's materials, or are merely possible Paleo-Indian sites lacking diagnostic artifacts but sharing non-diagnostic traits with 6LF21.

Although this site is very small in square meters of occupation, the concentration and diversity of artifacts (summarized in Table 16 and Fig. 10) are comparable to any Paleo-Indian site in the Eastern United States. In addition to the concentration and diversity of artifacts; the soil stratigraphy; the association of the artifacts with manufacturing debris and with the cobble layer; the fitting artifacts found horizontally displaced only a slight distance from one another; and the similarity of functional sections of each artifact type support the contention that this is a single, undisturbed, short-term Paleo-Indian occupation.

The similarity of tool types and the temporal proximity of acceptable carbon-14 dates from Paleo-Indian sites in the Northeast place 6LF21 comfortably with them. This permits an extrapolation of data from one site to all others in developing theoretical models to be applied in future excavations. One important relationship which must be explored in greater detail is that of man and the environment. To understand the true nature of the physical environment is to better understand the problems facing man in his cultural evolution and adaptation.

The scant clues from charcoal identified as red oak and either juniper or white cedar, cast Paleo-Indian in an environment quite different from the stereotypic tundra-taiga of the comic books and the spruce-pine forests of current theory. While the dominant land cover over hundreds or thousands of square miles may be hypothesized from pollen cores in bogs, the environment within which the

85

people were actually living can be understood only from an analysis of ecofacts excavated from their occupation areas. Since man is not living in general, but rather in specific econiches, charcoal, seeds, and bones from undisturbed occupation zones are crucial to accurate understanding.

A second aspect of the environmental picture is the role of currently extinct mammals, especially mammoth and mastodon. Although they have never been found in association with man's tools, or in circumstances suggesting man butchered or even hunted them in the Eastern United States, the possibility is still touted as a near certainty with only the vagaries of preservation precluding an absolute certainty. The majority of carbon-14 dates for these animals predate the Paleo-Indian sites, although the known sites are never spatially far from known mammoth or mastodon finds. Man had the same type fluted points in the Eastern United States that are found lodged in mammoth or mastodon kills in the West. Could man have ignored a chance to obtain food for the whole band for a week if he were to kill one of these prehistoric elephants?

However, archaeologists should not pass up the opportunity to learn of the lesser animals and plants which undoubtedly accounted for his more dependable and regular fare. This alone is sufficient reason that Paleo-Indian sites must be found and carefully excavated using the most precise techniques possible to recover the tiny carbonized clues to human diet: seeds and bones.

Paleo-Indian is the oldest culture in the United States for which extensive remains exist, but it is also the one for which the greatest information has yet to be found. This apparent dilemma results from the history of Paleo-Indian in the archaeological record. With all other time periods or cultures in the East, the first areas in which they were found were the areas immediately subjected to the greatest scrutiny by scientists, as well as pothunters. Both will destroy a site. One will use the best techniques of the time and save everything. The other will save only what is of interest and never record a thing. The bottom line is the same; even as techniques improve and new types of data are recognized and new analyses are conducted, old sites can never be re-dug.

Paleo-Indian is unique in that the first sites found were in the places most subject to disturbance and with the least likelihood for a full, detailed interpretation. Subsequently, sites were sought in similar areas. However, the good sites are not where they are likely to be disturbed. They are not in the places where people have been led to believe they ''had'' to be.

It is my sincere hope that anyone working with Paleo-Indian sites and artifacts consider the questions and their implications raised herein. While the data may be subject to other interpretations, it is the questions raised that are of lasting importance, not just the answers from a single site.

STATISTICAL SUMMARY AND DISCUSSION

The use, misuse, and abuse of statistics has been a topic in the majority of current archaeological publications. Although it is in vogue to use statistics to "prove" various hypotheses or to "discover" something that lay hidden in the data, most of this use is actually abuse. The assumption implicit in the more exotic number-crunching is that the further one gets from the actual specimens by quantifying them in all possible ways, the greater the likelihood of discovering something that was not seen with the naked eye. This criticism applies most to morphological traits, rather than the distribution of similar artifacts. Distribution studies should succeed the morphological and function studies describing and perhaps explaining why certain things are found where they are. For an excellent summary of the use, misuse, and abuse of statistics read a recent article by David Thomas (1978:231-44). This chapter will discuss the quantifications used in this book, as well as other current attempts to describe or explain Paleo-Indian data.

The primary function of the statistics in this book is to describe the quantity of data not described individually (debitage) and the relationships which exist between and among artifact categories and to summarize everything quantified. To facilitate comparisons, quantifications appear in the Tables. Many more comparisons are possible than those discussed here, but these were selected for specific reasons apparent in the text.

The distribution of flint chips by count (Table 1, Fig. 8) in each level of each square and totaled by level, by square, and for the entire site exhibits certain important relationships. With very few minor exceptions the count of flint chips increases level by level in each square by depth until it reaches a maximum point at which it begins to decrease. The same relationship holds if the total count for all levels is compared. This table merely shows that the relationship exists but does not explain why, nor does it prove the hypothesis that artifacts from single component sites will gradually move vertically upward or downward if left undisturbed for a sufficient period of time. However, it does provide a direction for future research and hypotheses.

The distribution of flint chips by weight (Table 2, Fig. 9) in each level of each square and totaled by level, by square, and for the entire site exhibits the same general tendencies as the chippage counts but with more exceptions. This is because of the difference in quantification caused by the diverse nature of the individual chips. With a count one chip is counted as any other one, only once. But with weights, heavier individual specimens contribute more to the total than lighter ones. The difference is due to chunks, trimming flakes, bifacial thinning flakes, and tiny retouch flakes being counted equally, but differing in size and, therefore, weight.

One might compare the count of flint chips in a given level and/or square to its weight to determine consistencies (Table 17). The absence of consistencies shows that the weight of a given collection of chips cannot be used to predict the number of chips it contains. This is because apples are being compared to oranges, tomatoes and elephants. Unless identical units are being compared, no comparisons should be attempted.

A weight/count (or average weight) table is totally unnecessary since a cursory visual inspection of the chippage would show that they not only differ in size, but also the manufacturing stage at which they were flaked from the core. Of course they are going to be different. The weight and count taken separately show the relative concentrations of debitage in different provenience units. But they cannot be combined to show the average weight of an individual chip.

The only way to show the relative weight of chips is to weigh each one. Depending upon the weight range and the distribution of weights in that range, the mean (average) may or may not be an appropriate statistic to describe that specific cluster. A huge chunk found in the same level with a pile of tiny retouching flakes is a perfect example of the necessity for segregating the different types of chippage prior to a statistical description comparing the contents of one unit with those of another. It also would be an excellent argument against using the mean to describe this cluster.

Tables 3, 4 and Figs. 8, 9 show the distribution of quartz chips by count and by weight for each level in each square and totalled by levels, by squares, and for the entire site. The absence of consistency in these Tables and Figures is just as important as the consistencies seen in the flint distribution. The presence of quartz within the component cannot be denied, but the distribution is very spotty and never in great quantity. It does not seem to be associated with the quartz tools either.

In this instance the presence and distribution of an artifact category generates more problems and more hypotheses than it answers. Could all of the quartz have been intrusive due to settling from subsequent occupations which used quartz almost exclusively? A visual analysis showed that most of the chips were very small, with occasional larger chunks, but this does not further the explanation for the distribution.

The last example of a distributional nature at the site is the location of discarded artifacts and bifacial thinning flakes by square and by level (Fig. 10). Although similar artifacts do not cluster, there is a general relationship between the bifacial thinning flakes and the discarded artifacts. The relationship seen in Fig. 8 between counts of flint chips and bifacial thinning flakes continues when discarded artifacts are added for consideration. If it were not known that the large numbers of flint chips included evidence of all stages of manufacture and retouch, the inference could never have been made that this was a manufacturing area where the finished tools were also utilized and then discarded. These Figures merely show the distribution of the different tools and chippage which had been previously categorized.

Graphs explicitly show relationships between two variables, but must be carefully examined to determine precisely what those relationships actually mean. Fig. 14 is a cumulative frequency graph showing the percentage of flint flakes in each level of the entire site. The relative steepness of the line between any pair of points reflects the percentage increase in the number of flakes. The steeper the line, the greater the percentage increase in flakes compared to previous and subsequent levels. The consistent increase without straight line plateaus, which would have indicated an absence of flakes in a particular level, is more obvious in this presentation than it would have been in a simple table.

The percentage of the total number of flakes in each level is very easy to find by dividing the total number of flakes in the sample (7229) into the number from each level. The three flakes from level 13 are .04% of the total; seven from level 12, .1%. This type of graph shows the percentage of the total number of flakes which have been found by the completion of the excavation of the entire level. Only .04% were found in level 13 and .1% were added from level 12 giving a total of .14% recovered upon completion of the second level into the component. The amount added in each succeeding level can be seen at a glance. A mere 10% of the flint flakes was found by the completion of level 6, but level 5 alone added 10% and level 4 accounted for nearly another 20%.

The technical error in using a cumulative frequency graph to show these data is that they are discontinuous. While it is possible to interpolate to find precisely the percentage increase from one level to the next, the same is not true of each individual level. One cannot say that 50% of the flint flakes had been recovered by the time the excavation had reached the middle of level 3. Since the information was recorded by full levels and not by fractions of levels, no interpolation within a level is permitted on this graph.

The use of a smooth curve should indicate that the observations were made at every point along the line, or that interpolation is permitted to determine the correct observations. In this case the smooth curve was a more convenient way to show the relationships than a bar graph (histogram), which would have had extremely tiny bars lost next to outrageously large ones. The true nature of the vertical distributions would have been more difficult to discern.

On the other hand, the slight variation in the bifacial thinning flake weights from value to value and the frequent gaps between values at the maximum end of the range is more appropriately shown in a bar graph (Fig. 12). The number of flakes of each weight can be seen, as can the clustering of flakes with similar weights. The very tight clustering of values is what would be expected of flakes being struck at the same stage of manufacture. Had a study been done of the retouching flakes, a similar type of distribution would be expected.

Once the simple distributional tables and figures were completed, several interesting correlations seemed to be present. Bifacial thinning flake count totals in each square seemed to increase directly with the flint chip counts. While this is an obvious correlation from an examination of Fig. 8, the actual strength of this correlation can be measured statistically.

Spearman's Rho is a rank order statistical correlation test (Blalock 1972:416-8). Table 18 shows the flint chip and bifacial thinning flake count for each square in the Paleo-Indian component. Each square is then ranked for flint chip count and bifacial thinning flake count with the greatest count being assigned the number (1). Ties are averaged. The difference between the flint chip and bifacial thinning flake rank (D) is obtained and then squared (D^2). The sum of the squares (ΣD^2) is inserted into the mathematical formula with the number of units of observation (N).

The formula has been designed to yield a number ranging from zero to one, with zero suggesting a very poor correlation and one a perfect correlation between the two variables. The correlation between the flint chips and bifacial thinning flake counts is very high, but the strength of the correlation (level of significance) can also be measured. The formula for measuring the strength of the rank order correlation (Table 18) uses Z. The very high value for Z means that most of the difference between the two variables has been explained (Blalock 1972: Table C). The value of .0004652 is the level of significance or amount of unexplained difference. This is an exceedingly low value and indicates an extremely strong relationship between the two variables.

The implication of this correlation is that bifacial thinning flakes are closely associated with the rest of the debitage. This is a reasonable conclusion since the manufacturing process proceeds from core reduction through trimming, bifacial thinning, and finally to retouching. If all of these activities occur in the same place, all of the debris will be deposited together and will remain in close proximity unless disturbed.

Thus far three distributional studies have shown or at least suggested that the site has not been extensively disturbed and that its artifacts and debitage resulted from a single occupation: flint chip counts, flint chip weights, and the association of flint chips with bifacial thinning flakes by inspection of the Figures and by rank order correlation. The tight clustering of bifacial thinning flake weights may also be considered to reflect similar motor habits and optimum size of flake to be removed.

A much stronger statistical test than the graphs and Tables and even the rank order correlation is the product-moment correlation, the reason being that rank order correlations are just simple rankings. In the example from this site a rank of (1) for the flint represents an actual count of 2552, while the rank of (1) for bifacial thinning flakes represents 86. A lot of information might be lost by too much number-crunching or summarizing.

The product-moment correlation uses the actual counts (Table 19). The flint chip count (X) for each square is multiplied by the bifacial thinning flake count (Y). The flint chip count and bifacial thinning flake count are each squared (X^2, Y^2). The total flint chip count, bifacial thinning flake count, product of flint chip and bifacial thinning flake counts (XY), and squares of the flint chip and bifacial thinning flake counts are each summed separately (ΣX, ΣY, ΣXY, ΣX^2, ΣY^2). These numbers are then inserted into the formula for r (Table 19).

Blalock (1972:376-83) discusses the meaning of the product-moment correlation (r) as a measure of dispersion about the linear least-squares equation. For the non-statistician this means the amount of variation from a straight line. Had the relationship been perfectly linear, an increase in X would yield an increase in Y. If that had been the case, r would be (1) showing that there was a perfect correlation. A (− 1) would have meant a perfect negative correlation, showing an increase in X yields a decrease in Y. As the number of instances in which certain values are not on the line increases, the value of r decreases. When r reaches zero, there is no linear relationship whatsoever. But there may be curvilinear relationships in which X increases as Y increases until a point is reached beyond which X continues to increase as Y decreases.

The value for r in the correlation between flint chip count and bifacial thinning flake count is very high (Table 19), indicating that a very strong relationship exists between them. This may be due to a pair of very high values (2466 and 86), far greater than the second highest (865 and 28). To test for a statistical anomaly due to a single value skewing the results, these values are dropped and r is recomputed. The correlation decreases, but stays high (Table 19).

The only drawback to the use of the product-moment correlation in this example is that it is totally inappropriate. The variables are not linear. Had they been linear, a single value for flint chip count would have corresponded to a single value for bifacial thinning flakes. It does not. Two bifacial thinning flakes correspond to 8, 38, 51, and 96 flint chips. A simple graph (technically a scattergram) showing flint count corresponding to bifacial thinning flake count demonstrates that the dots are not even close to being connected by a single straight line. It is not possible to draw a single line coming as close to all of the dots as is indicated by the extremely high correlation from the formula. The formula is not at fault, the test was inappropriately applied.

There is disagreement about how non-linear the relationship must be before this statistical correlation test can no longer be applied. A conservative approach would be to plot all of the values on a graph and examine the dispersion. If the dots cluster about a straight line without having extreme gaps between adjacent values, and without having a few extreme values widely separated from the primary cluster, then the relationship is linear. If the points are vastly divergent or if there are several possible lines about which a cluster is found, then the relationship is probably not linear. Of course, the larger the sample, the greater the likelihood of seeing a pattern.

An additional problem in using these types of statistical tests based upon the correlation between different categories (types) of artifacts is that the original unit of observation is not cultural, but arbitrary. I can say without fear of contradiction that the inhabitants of 6LF21 did not deposit these artifacts within the confines of a 1.5m square corresponding to the 1.5m squares of the excavation. The arbitrary selection of that unit is in effect a sampling unit created by the archaeologist from which cultural interpretations are made.

Had the 1.5m squares been aligned differently or had 1m squares been used for the excavation, the quantity of flint chips and bifacial thinning flakes per unit would have been different. The unanswerable question is, would the relationship seen in this analysis have been the same? Would there have been a strong correlation per excavation unit for the two had the units of observation been different?

This question could have been answered had the position of every single piece of stone been plotted during the excavation. Since the positions of all artifacts and debitage could have been plotted in three dimensional space, a computer program could be written to illustrate the true associations of the artifacts. The association between the chippage and the bifacial thinning flakes would then have more closely approximated their original distribution than the arbitrary 5cm levels and 1.5m squares. Going one step further the simulation could then show which combinations of level thickness and square dimensions could have been employed to yield most nearly the same results.

Computer simulations of this type were employed in a large-scale excavation at Shawnee-Minisink. They are extremely time-consuming not only in the excavation phase, but in analysis, computer programing, and interpretation. While they could be invaluable in resolving this case, there is no guarantee that a given site excavated under these conditions will yield sufficient high-quality data to make the effort worthwhile.

STATISTICAL COMPARISONS TO OTHER SITES

Although the sizes of the excavation areas varied at Debert, this is not important for purposes of comparison. Table 21 compares the distribution of artifacts from each of the excavation areas at Debert (MacDonald 1968: Table 3 translated from percentages to counts) to 6LF21. The point being emphasized is that there are important similarities and differences between 6LF21 and each area at Debert, which MacDonald considered to be a separate camp.

The most striking difference is the absence at Debert of several functional categories: graving spurs, knives, and miniature points. No channel flakes are mentioned, but these might have been included with debitage. The huge quantity of utilized flakes, retouched flakes, and pièces esquillées (wedges used for bone or wood splitting) at Debert is also a marked difference. The last difference is the number of scrapers relative to the remaining categories of artifacts.

Looking at these differences and bearing in mind the hypothesis that 6LF21 is a short-term, single occupation site, the only reasonable conclusion is that the Debert sections are not individual camps of short duration. The preponderance of scrapers suggests a specialized functional area for processing large quantities of something. In the absence of a detailed microwear analysis, but given the probable presence of caribou and the northern climate, hide processing and butchering is an obvious, necessary function to suggest.

Following the specialized-hide-processing-and-butchering-camp hypothesis further, one is struck by the abundance of pick-up tools such as utilized waste flakes. Recent work by Phillip Walker has shown that "if cutting effectiveness were the only criterion used by prehistoric hunters in tool selection, flakes with unmodified working edges would have been the preferred tool for many butchering tasks" (1978:714). The only problem is that they have a relatively short functional life and then must be either retouched or discarded. This would explain the presence of so many retouched waste flakes. The pieces esquillées would have been used to split the bone for marrow, to obtain splinters for tools (awls or needles), or even to assist in disarticulating the skeleton of the caribou. The gravers would have been employed in the final stages of removing appropriate pieces of bone from the splinters for further working.

The paucity of bifacial rejects indicates very little bifacial tool manufacturing. Table 21 shows the extremely high proportion of artifacts to debitage and the paucity of debitage in actual count, and relative to the size of the area excavated in comparison to 6LF21. All of this strongly suggests that Debert's separate sections were highly specialized work areas where very little manufacturing of stone tools was occurring.

West Athens Hill near Albany and Twin Fields near Wallkill, New York, are also compared to 6LF21 in Table 20 only to show how the artifact and chippage density per square meter and artifact chippage ratios compare. Since The West Athens Hill site is on a flint quarry, one would expect a very heavy concentration of debitage per square foot. Although it is greater than at 6LF21, the similarity is obvious. The quantity of chippage relative to the number of finished artifacts is extremely small. Comparisons to each separate section at Debert also give the impression of how densely packed the artifacts and chippage were at 6LF21.

The preceding statistical discussion may seem overdrawn and pedantic, but it was included for a reason. The best use of statistics in archaeology is to describe the data. If the statistical tests, graphs, tables, and figures do not describe, they are worthless. It is from the careful description of the data that correct interpretations and comparisons come.

IF I HAD IT ALL TO DO OVER

During the years since the excavation, I have been asked frequently what would I do differently if I had known exactly what was there. I am certain that every archaeologist has wrestled with this question, but few ever publicly announce their intentions.

If I had it all to do over and knew exactly what I was going to find, I would have mapped every single artifact, flake, and stone *in situ* using a coordinate system and precise depths below datum. A microtopographic map of the surface of the clay-coated sand layer would have been done to show more precisely the surface contours of the Paleo-Indian component.

Aside from those changes in the excavation plan, I would have changed nothing about the way in which the dig was conducted. The crew was excellent in all regards. The thought of a field school with total novices is enough to bring sweat to the archaeologist's brow in a blizzard, unless it was the kind of group we had in 1977. Despite the close analysis of artifacts, maps, and other data from the excavation, I was unable to find conflicting, totally outrageous, or incompetently recorded information. Of course, part of the success of the field school participants has to be attributed to the close attention and training given by the staff. The students provided the personal motivation and perseverance in the face of unfamiliar, adverse conditions. A paid professional crew would have been able to move more dirt and recognize a larger number of artifacts *in situ,* but given the same excavation plan, could not have recorded their findings more accurately.

Mapping of every single artifact and flake before removal would have permitted much more detailed distribution maps, which would have provided more information concerning clusters of debitage and artifacts. While it is known that the bifacial thinning flakes were found in the same levels as the majority of the artifacts, it would have been more meaningful to show a distribution map with a small cluster of bifacial thinning flakes of the same colored and textured flint as adjacent retouching flakes and finished artifacts. While the case can be made that the site is a single component occupied for a short period of time without very much post-depositional disturbance, proof could have been found in the distribution maps showing fitting fragments of chips laying only a few centimeters apart.

The microtopographic map of the surface of the Paleo-Indian component in conjunction with the precise depth and coordinate map would have been useful in segregating potentially intrusive artifacts, especially the quartz ones. During the excavation an abrupt change from one depositional layer to the next was evident. While the vertical wall profiles show this distinction, the exact point of distinction cannot be reconstructed for an area that is one meter from the wall. The undulating surface of the stratigraphic layer could have been recognized easily, uncovered, and mapped using the transit and stadia rod. While the level above the clay-coated sand was usually culturally sterile, the few artifacts present could have settled into the deeper levels.

These techniques would not have changed the interpretation of the vast majority of the data. They would have cleared up the minor fringes, added a bit more support to certain ideas or suggested interpretations, but I cannot think of how they might have permitted a definite conclusion which was not suggested by existing data. However, I could be wrong. Once a technique is applied consistently and the results are analyzed, the interpretation of its efficacy should be made. With more precise data new associations may have become evident.

The use of flotation is another case in point. The flotation done at this site did not reveal anything that we did not already have or suspect. Charcoal and minute retouching flakes were found in all of the samples in varying quantities. Had flotation been done consistently on the same sized sample from every single level and square, more data would have been obtained. The utility of these data in making assumptions beyond those made already is dubious. Given the manpower and the time required for processing with little hope of significant results, I think I would pass it up the second time. If circumstances would have permitted seed or bone preservation, flotation would have been an essential procedure.

The analysis of the data will never cease. There are so many avenues open that I have not delved into in this study. A detailed analysis of the chippage has yet to be done. An expert knapper who has studied his own chippage, Errett Callahan, notes many consistencies in his own work. The concept of each knapper having idiosyncratic patterning could be explored here. Although no one can assume that a single knapper is responsible for all of the debitage at the site, the probability exists that only a few people are responsible. Can this similarity in workmanship be detected and ascribed to a minimum number of workers? Is it possible that a lifetime of practice in conjunction with a limited number of alternative means of knapping flint and knapping in small groups will yield a collection of debitage which cannot be segregated according to the number of people who made it?

The close analysis of every single flake according to striking platform preparation, bulb of percussion, ripple marks, stress cracks, length, width, thickness, weight, etc. by an experienced lithics analyst will reveal manufacturing procedures, techniques, and problems. While Callahan's study (1979) of the Williamson site shows the techniques of these knappers in the Middle Atlantic area, it would be interesting to see if the knappers of the Shepaug were similar in any or all regards. There are certain necessary points of similarity only because of the nature of the materials being worked, but the selection of the same optional or selective techniques would be very interesting. Not only would the intra-site comparison be instructive, but also the inter-site comparisons among the many Paleo-Indian sites in the Northeast and Eastern United States.

SELECTED REFERENCES

Adovasio, J., J.D. Gunn, J. Donahue, and R. Stuckenrath
    1977   Meadowcroft Rockshelter: Retrospect 1976. *Pennsyl-
            vania Archaeologist* 47(2-3).
Bernabo, J.C. and T. Webb
    1977   Changing Patterns in the Holocene Pollen Record of
            Northeastern North America: A Mapped Summary.
            Quaternary Research 8:64-96.
Blalock, Hubert
    1972   *Social Statistics,* second edition. McGraw Hill,
            New York.
Brink, John W.
    1978   *An Experimental Study of Microwear Formation on End-
            scrapers.* National Museum of Man Mercury Series.
            Archaeological Survey of Canada Paper No. 83.
            Ottawa.
Callahan, Errett
    1979   The Basics of Biface Knapping in the Eastern Fluted
            Point Tradition: A Manual for Flintknappers and Lithic
            Analysts. *Archaeology of Eastern North America*
            7:1-180.
Cook, Frederick B.
    1978   The Finding of the Farmington Valley Mastodon.
            Artifacts 7(2):8-10.
Cox, Steven
    1972   A Re-Analysis of the Shoop Site. Department of Anthro-
            pology, Smithsonian Institution, Washington, D.C.
Dragoo, Christine
    1979   The Proboscidians and Man. *Archaeology of Eastern
            North America* 7:180-213.
Dragoo, Don
    1974   Radiocarbon-14 Dates and the Archaeologist.
            Archaeology of Eastern North America 2:21-29.
Eisenberg, Leonard
    1978   *Paleo-Indian Settlement Pattern in the Hudson and
            Delaware River Drainages.* Occasional Publications in
            Northeastern Anthropology, No. 4.
Fagan, Lisa
    1978   A Vegetational and Cultural Sequence for Southern New
            England 15,000 B.P. to 7000 B.P. *Man in the North-
            east* 15-16:70-92.
Funk, Robert
    1972   Early Man in the Northeast and the Late-Glacial
            Environment. *Man in the Northeast* 4:7-39.

99

1976   *Recent Contributions to Hudson Valley Prehistory.*
       New York State Museum and Science Service Memoir 22.

1977   Early Cultures in the Hudson Drainage Basin. In
       Amerinds and Their Paleoenvironments in Northeastern
       North America (Newman and Salwen, eds). pp. 316-32.

1978   Post-Pleistocene Adaptations. In *Handbook of North*
       American Indians, Vol. 15 (Trigger, ed). pp. 16-19.

Funk, Robert and Charles Hayes, III, eds.
1977   *Current Perspectives in Northeastern Archeology.*
       New York State Archaeological Association, Albany.

Funk, Robert, Thomas Weinman, and Paul L. Weinman
1969   The Kings Road Site: A Recently Discovered Paleo-
       Indian Manifestation in Greene County, New York.
       New York State Archaeological Association Bulletin
       45:1-23.

Gardner, William M.
1974   The Flint Run Complex: Pattern and Process During
       the Paleo-Indian to Early Archaic. In *The Flint Run*
       Paleo-Indian Complex: A Preliminary Report 1971-73
       Seasons (Gardner, ed). pp. 5-47.

1977   Flint Run Paleoindian Complex and its Implications
       for Eastern North American Prehistory. In *Amerinds*
       and Their Paleoenvironments in Northeastern North
       America (Newman and Salwen, eds). pp. 257-63.

Gardner, William M., ed.
1974   *The Flint Run Paleo-Indian Complex: A Preliminary*
       Report 1971-73 Seasons. Occasional Publication No.
       1, Department of Anthropology, The Catholic Univer-
       sity of America, Washington, D.C.

Gardner, William and Robert Verrey
1979   Typology and Chronology of Fluted Points from the
       Flint Run Area. *Pennsylvania Archaeologist*
       49(1-2):13-46.

Gonick, Walter, Arthur Shearin, and David Hill
1970   *Soil Survey of Litchfield County, Connecticut.*
       United States Department of Agriculture. Government
       Printing Office, Washington, D.C.

Guilday, John
1969   A Possible Caribou-Paleo-Indian Association from
       Dutchess Quarry Cave, Orange County, New York. *New*
       York State Archaeological Association Bulletin
       45:24-29.

Handsman, Russell, ed.
1978   *Hunters and Gatherers, Villages and Farms: A Preser-*
       vation Plan for Litchfield County's Past. Report to
       the Connecticut Historical Commission.

Hodson, F.R.
1971   Numerical Typology and Prehistoric Archaeology. In

       Mathematics in the Archaeological and Historical Sciences (Hodson, Kendall, and Tautu, eds). pp. 30-45.

Hodson, F.R., D.G. Kendall, and P. Tautu, eds.
    1971   *Mathematics in the Archaeological and Historical Sciences*. Aldine, Chicago.

Jennings, Jesse
    1974   *Prehistory of North America*, revised edition. McGraw-Hill, New York.

Jordon, Douglas
    1960   *The Bull Brook Site in Relation to "Fluted Point" Manifestations in Eastern North America*. Unpublished Ph.D. dissertation, Harvard University.

Kauffman, Barbara and Joseph Dent
    1978   Preliminary Flora and Fauna Recovery and Analysis at the Shawnee-Minisink Site (36 MR 43). Paper presented at the Ninth Middle Atlantic Conference on March 19th.

Kraft, Herbert
    1973   The Plenge Site: A Paleo-Indian Occupation Site in New Jersey. *Archaeology of Eastern North America* 1:56-117.
    1977   The Paleo-Indian Sites at Port Mobil, Staten Island. In *Current Perspectives in Northeastern Archaeology* (Funk and Hayes, eds). pp. 1-19.

MacDonald, George
    1968   *Debert: A Paleo-Indian Site in Central Nova Scotia*. National Museum of Canada Anthropological Paper 16.

McNett, Charles, Barbara McMillan, and Sydne B. Marshall
    1977   The Shawnee-Minisink Site. In *Amerinds and Their Paleoenvironments in Northeastern North America* (Newman and Salwen, eds). pp. 282-96.

Newman, Walter S. and Bert Salwen, eds.
    1977   *Amerinds and Their Paleoenvironments in Northeastern North America*. Annals of the New York Academy of Sciences Vol. 288.

Ogden, J. Gordon, III
    1977   The Late Quaternary Paleoenvironmental Record of Northeastern North America. In *Amerinds and Their Paleoenvironments in Northeastern North America* (Newman and Salwen, eds). pp. 16-34.

Painter, Floyd
    1974   The Cattail Creek Fluting Tradition and its Complex-Determining Lithic Debris. *The American Archaeologist* 1(1):20-32.

Park, Edwards
    1978   The Ginsberg Caper: Hacking it as in Stone Age. *Smithsonian* 9(4):85-96.

Patton, Peter
    1978   The Fluvial Geology of the Housatonic River
           Drainage System. In *Hunters and Gatherers,*
           Villages and Farms: A Preservation Plan for
           Litchfield County's Past (Handsman, ed). pp.
           45-55.
Ralph, Elizabeth, H.N. Michael, and M.C. Han
    1974   Radiocarbon Dates and Reality. *Archaeology of*
           Eastern North America 2:1-20.
Rippeteau, Bruce
    1974   Using C-14 Calendrical Corrections and Conven-
           tions. *Archaeology of Eastern North America*
           2:29-37.
Ritchie, William A.
    1965   *The Archaeology of New York State.* Natural
           History Press, Garden City.
Ritchie, William A. and Robert Funk
    1973   *Aboriginal Settlement Patterns in the Northeast.*
           New York State Museum and Science Service
           Memoir 20.
Semenov, S.A.
    1964   *Prehistoric Technology* (Thompson, translator).
           Harper and Row, New York.
Thomas, David
    1978   The Awful Truth About Statistics in Archaeology.
           American Antiquity 43:231-44.
Trigger, Bruce, ed.
    1978   *Handbook of North American Indians, Volume 15.*
           Smithsonian Institution, Washington, D.C.
Walker, Phillip L.
    1978   Butchering and Stone Tool Function. *American*
           Antiquity 43:710-5.
Wiegand, Ernest A.
    1979   The Lake Kitchawan Mastodon Dig. *Artifacts*
           7(4):4.
Wilmsen, Edwin
    1970   *Lithic Analysis and Cultural Inference: A Paleo-*
           Indian Case. Anthropological Papers of the
           University of Arizona Number 16.
    1974   *Lindenmeier: A Pleistocene Hunting Society.*
           Harper and Row, New York.
Witthoft, John
    1952   A Paleo-Indian Site in Eastern Pennsylvania.
           Proceedings of the American Philosophical Society
           96(4):464-95.
Wormington, H.M.
    1964   *Ancient Man in North America,* revised edition.
           Denver Museum of Natural History, Denver.

APPENDIX A

Attributes Used in Artifact Analysis

I.   Tool Category
    A. Bifacial thinning flake
    B. Utilized waste flake
    C. Finished tools (retouched, reworked included)

II.   Flaking Traits
    A. Type of flake
        1. Cortical: any trace of cortex remaining
        2. Primary: first flakes removed from decorticated core
        3. Trimming: all flakes removed subsequent to primary ones
    B. Nature of detachment
        1. Bulb of percussion
           a. presence/absence
           b. relative size
        2. Bulbar scars: presence/absence
        3. Ripple marks or concentric rings
           a. presence/absence
           b. relative size and spacing
    C. Heat treatment
        1. Discoloration
        2. Pot lids

III.   Striking Platform Characteristics
    A. Preparation
        1. Flat: no preparation
        2. Transverse retouch: from dorsal to ventral face
        3. Lateral retouch: from lateral to lateral
        4. Abraded: roughened with no individual scars evident
        5. Combinations of the first four
        6. Indeterminate: striking platform absent
    B. Transverse length: measured from dorsal to ventral at top of platform
    C. Lateral length: measured from lateral to lateral at top of platform
    D. Platform angle: angle between surface of striking platform and ventral face
    E. Bulb thickness: maximum thickness measured dorsal to ventral

Note: All measurements are actual, none based upon reconstructions.

IV.   Geometry of Entire Specimen
    A. Length: measured perpendicular to striking platform
    B. Width: measured perpendicular to length at widest point
    C. Thickness: measured below bulb of percussion
    D. Maximum width position: widest point on specimen
        1. Proximal: end with striking platform
        2. Distal: end opposite striking platform
        3. Midpoint
        4. Between midpoint and proximal
        5. Between distal and midpoint
    E. Length to maximum width: measured from distal end to widest point
    F. Length to maximum thickness: measured from distal end to thickest point (excluding bulb of percussion)
    G. Weight

Note: If the striking platform had been destroyed, measurements were made with respect to where it was without allowing for the amount destroyed. The determination of where it was was based upon any remaining traces of the platform itself, ripple marks, bulbar scars, or other traits. Bifacially worked specimens were arbitrarily oriented with the functional end (tip) designated as distal.

V.   Shape and Cross Section
   A.   Lateral outline: shown in photographs
         (Had photographs not been made of all specimens, the
         outline would have been described by quadrant as con-
         vex, concave, or straight.)
   B.   Lateral cross section: as viewed from proximal end
         with dorsal face given first, followed by ventral. Dor-
         sal is the most flaked face usually. On a biface dorsal
         would be the best face or obverse. Ventral is the un-
         modified face of a uniface, the reverse, or the face
         with the bulb of percussion, ripple marks, or bulbar
         scars from the initial detachment from the core or
         primary flakes.
         1.   Convex
         2.   Concave
         3.   Plano
   C.   Longitudinal cross section: as viewed from the longer
         lateral with dorsal face on the left and given first,
         followed by ventral
         1.   Convex
         2.   Concave
         3.   Plano

VI.   Retouch or Utilization Characteristics
   A.   Face on which it occurs
         1.   Dorsal
         2.   Ventral
         3.   Both
   B.   Lateral or end on which it occurs
         1.   Left
         2.   Right
         3.   Proximal
         4.   Distal
*Note: Face must also be recorded to differentiate left lateral retouch
(dorsal) from left lateral retouch (ventral).*

   C.   Edge angle: On all artifacts this is the angle between
         the dorsal and ventral faces. On utilized/retouched
         flakes this includes only utilized/retouched portions.
   D.   Multiple functions: These observations are reported
         for each section with differences in retouch or utiliza-
         tion, i.e. gravers on scrapers would be recorded
         separately.

105

VII.   Wear Patterns: do not include steps in manufacturing, but
       do include cause for rejection of bifaces
       A.   Polish
       B.   Striations
       C.   Impact fractures
       D.   Hinge fractures
       E.   Step fractures
       F.   Nibbling
Note: Each is located according to face and to lateral.

VIII. Fluted Points
       A.   Basal width: measured from ear to ear
       B.   Flute width
            1.   Obverse
            2.   Reverse
       C.   Number of flutes struck
            1.   Obverse
            2.   Reverse
       D.   Flute length
            1.   Obverse
            2.   Reverse

MODIFIED FROM COX (1972) and WILMSEN (1970, 1974)

APPENDIX B

TABLES   FIGURES   PLATES

In a deliberate departure from the common practice all of the Tables, Figures, and Plates have been put into a single section.

TABLES

1-4   Square 4.5N1.5W had no flint chips and no artifacts which could be considered Paleo-Indian. It also had no cobbles (Fig. 7). Square 4.5N3.OW is only partially within the cobble area and had only a single flint chip, one quartz chip, and no Paleo-Indian artifacts. For these reasons 4.5N1.5W is considered outside of the area of occupation, and 4.5N3.OW is on the border.

5-15   Provenience measurements are in meters below datum. Artifact measurements are in centimeters and grams. Lateral and longitudinal cross section: Convex (Cvx), Concave (Cnv), and Plano give the dorsal shape followed by the ventral. Angles are expressed as the range for the normal edge excluding extraordinary bulges or concavities. Characteristics of the striking platform are given for artifacts made from flakes: Abraded (Abr), Transversely flaked (Trans), Laterally flaked (Lat), Crushed (Crsh). Multiple styles of platform preparation were observed on bifacial thinning flakes but not on other artifacts. Edge wear is summarized briefly: Erratic nicking and/or nibbling (E), Nibbled (N), Nicks (Ni), Polish (P).

18-19   Square 4.5N3.OW has been omitted, since its inclusion would have skewed the results. Although the interpretation of the statistics would not have changed drastically in this case, the potential skewing effect must be noted for future applications.

20   Cores have been included as large bifacial rejects.

FIGURES

3-6 The vertical white space having two square numbers (4.5N4.5W and 6.ON4.5W) designates a break in the continuity of the profile. Since the excavated area was not a perfect rectangle but actually was made of several connected ones, the profiles are not continuous. A comparison of the profiles to the site plan (Fig. 2) will show where each segment of each profile is located. Vertical measurements are in centimeters above and below datum. Only the largest rocks found directly in the wall were mapped in the profiles. Since the profiles are at the periphery of the site, the cobbles are not as evident. The dotted line designating the deepest artifact level is an artist's rendition. The level for the deepest artifacts did not necessarily occur at the wall, nor was it continuous. The reason for terminating the excavation of a particular square at a certain depth was the presence of heavy gravel, cobbles, or both. The artifacts were usually found at the base of the clay-coated sand. But since this zone was not perfectly level across the site, the artifact bearing zone seems to continue into the mixture area. This was the case only rarely.

7 The entire cobble layer is shown with the addition of 4.5N1.5W which had no cobbles and no Paleo-Indian artifacts. Squares grid west of 6.0N9.OW are probably outside of the Paleo-Indian occupation area, at least in part. The cobbles disappear rapidly as do possible Paleo-Indian artifacts and debitage.

8-9 Counts and weights for flint, quartz, and bifacial thinning flakes are shown only for the first 10 levels. Tables 1-4 show the counts and weights for all 13 levels. Counts and weights of bifacial thinning flakes are already included with the counts and weights for flint flakes. There were no bifacial thinning flakes of quartz.

All of the pictured specimens are of flint, except for four quartz artifacts: scraper (Plate 11a), drill (Plates 12f, 15), retouched flake (Plate 20c), and hammerstone (Plate 21).

2 In the early phase of mapping a plumb bob is used to accurately pinpoint the location of each object within the grid. In this phase the mapped objects are being labeled and checked for accuracy.

3 The sprayer is used to carefully wet the soil prior to mapping to bring out the detail lost by dessication.

5-12, 16, 18-22 Provenience information is provided in detail with a complete metrical and attribute description in Tables 5-15.

15 The scale is in centimeters.

22 The flakes are being held on edge by small lumps of clay. Specimen C has apparently been utilized, but this cannot be stated with certainty. With such thin edges, utilization and edge damage due to trowel trauma, sifter shaking, artifact container movement, and four separate sortings of all artifacts can be confused.

LEVEL

Square Number	1	2	3	4	5	6	7	8	9	10	11	12	13	Square Total
4.5N3.0W	1													1
4.5N4.5W	1	3	3	1		1	1							10
6.0N1.5W	4	2	1	1	0									8
6.0N3.0W	1	2	10	9	6	1	4	1	0	2	0	1	1	38
6.0N4.5W	4	30	31	19	31	2	6	1						124
6.0N6.0W	58	137	156	130	87	24	9	1						602
6.0N7.5W	11	46	19	33	9	7	2	6	3					136
6.0N9.0W	22	29	92	19	9	1	4							176
7.5N1.5W	123	186	47	27	11	6	7	7	5	1	3	1		424
7.5N3.0W	0	212	415	118	78	33	15	9	3	7	0	1	2	893
7.5N4.5W	25	62	60	56	27	18	13	14						275
7.5N6.0W	245	730	591	527	233	98	67	31	19	11				2552
7.5N7.5W	21	126	185	94	39	16	10	9	17	16				533
7.5N9.0W	88	65	12	10	2	1	3	1						182
9.0N1.5W	23	71	29	11	10	2	5	1	2	1				155
9.0N3.0W	1	118	361	117	76	35	2	9	12	4	9	4		748
9.0N4.5W	5	3	5	9	13	7	6	1	2					51
9.0N6.0W	165	15	12	4	4	2	1	2	7	0	13			225
9.0N7.5W	15	14	14	10	10	0	8	5	6	10	4			96
Level Total	813	1851	2043	1195	645	254	163	98	76	52	29	7	3	

Grand Total 7229

TABLE 1. Flint Chip Count by Level for Each Square in the Paleo-Indian Component.

110

LEVEL

Square Number	1	2	3	4	5	6	7	8	9	10	11	12	13	Square Total
4.5N3.0W	.1													.1
4.5N4.5W	.5	1.1	2.5	.1	0	.2	.2							4.6
6.0N1.5W	.6	1.1	.2	.2										2.1
6.0N3.0W	.2	.4	2.4	2.2	5.1	.1	.9	.1	0	.4	0	.2	.2	12.2
6.0N4.5W	.9	16.9	14.1	7.2	11.7	.2	2.3	.2						53.5
6.0N6.0W	22.3	67.2	52.8	45.1	17.0	5.5	5.0	1.7						216.6
6.0N7.5W	3.6	11.3	6.5	9.7	1.6	1.4	.5	2.2	.7					37.5
6.0N9.0W	11.1	13.2	19.2	4.4	1.6	.2	1.3							51.0
7.5N1.5W	49.7	62.9	20.4	8.5	5.8	2.2	1.0	1.5	.8	.8	.6	.4		154.6
7.5N3.0W	0	59.2	120.3	33.5	21.8	8.7	5.6	1.6	.9	2.7	0	.2	.3	254.8
7.5N4.5W	7.7	31.9	20.3	27.0	14.5	3.7	10.2	2.5						117.8
7.5N6.0W	140.1	202.3	136.1	102.9	55.0	19.2	10.8	7.0	3.8	4.8				682.0
7.5N7.5W	5.7	41.4	76.1	22.4	7.9	2.5	3.0	2.9	2.7	5.6				170.2
7.5N9.0W	22.7	23.2	2.3	1.1	.2	.5	2.7	.1						52.8
9.0N1.5W	13.1	28.2	9.8	2.7	2.2	.6	2.0	.1	.9	.6				60.2
9.0N3.0W	1.1	35.1	74.4	48.8	30.0	10.0	4.4	2.4	3.3	.4	5.5	1.5		216.9
9.0N4.5W	5.5	1.3	2.9	1.5	2.6	8.7	1.0	.1	.7					24.3
9.0N6.0W	50.7	9.6	9.1	1.8	.8	2.2	.3	.5	2.2	0	18.7			95.9
9.0N7.5W	2.5	6.2	3.5	1.1	7.4	0	2.6	.4	11.0	17.3	.8			52.8
Level Total	338.1	612.5	572.9	320.2	185.2	65.9	53.8	23.3	27.0	32.6	25.6	2.3	.5	2259.9 gms

Grand Total 2259.9 gms

TABLE 2 . Flint Chip Weight by Level for Each Square in the Paleo-Indian Component.

111

LEVEL

Square Number	1	2	3	4	5	6	7	8	9	10	11	12	Square Total
4.5N3.0W		1											1
4.5N4.5W					3								3
6.0N1.5W				4									4
6.0N3.0W			1		1	1						3	6
6.0N4.5W							1						1
6.0N6.0W			2			1		2					5
6.0N7.5W							1						1
6.0N9.0W	1		1	1	2	1	4						10
7.5N1.5W									4			1	5
7.5N3.0W					4	9						2	15
7.5N4.5W						1	1						2
7.5N6.0W								6					6
7.5N7.5W					1		2						3
7.5N9.0W	2				4	1	1	3		2			13
9.0N1.5W								1				2	3
9.0N3.0W				2	1			2		1	2		8
9.0N4.5W									4				4
9.0N6.0W			1	2		1		2	2		6		14
9.0N7.5W			1	3	1	1	2	6		2	11	—	27
Level Total	3	1	6	12	17	16	12	22	10	5	19	8	

Grand Total   131

TABLE 3. Quartz Chip Counts by Level for Each Square in the Paleo-Indian Component.

112

LEVEL

TABLE 4. Quartz Chip Weight by Level for Each Square in the Paleo-Indian Component.

Square Number	1	2	3	4	5	6	7	8	9	10	11	12	Square Total
4.5N3.0W		1.1											1.1
4.5N4.5W					19.7								19.7
6.0N1.5W				1.1									1.1
6.0N3.0W			.3		.3	.4						.4	1.4
6.0N4.5W							.4						.4
6.0N6.0W			.8			2.1		3.0					5.9
6.0N7.5W							.9						.9
6.0N9.0W	.6		.6	.3	1.1	.1	3.0						5.7
7.5N1.5W									13.9			.1	14.0
7.5N3.0W					22.7	5.4						.4	28.5
7.5N4.5W						.1	.1						.2
7.5N6.0W								19.1					19.1
7.5N7.5W					.2					.9			1.1
7.5N9.0W	.9		.3	.2	.8		.4	1.0					3.6
9.0N1.5W						.2	16.8	.7					17.7
9.0N3.0W				.3				.1		.3	1.0	.8	2.5
9.0N4.5W					.2	.2		7.1					7.5
9.0N6.0W			10.5			.3		.5	1.3		4.8		17.4
9.0N7.5W				.6	2.9		.5	12.2	7.0	1.2	23.0		47.4
Level Total	1.5	1.1	12.5	2.5	47.9	8.8	22.1	43.7	22.2	2.4	28.8	1.7	

Grand Total 195.2 gms.

113

Specimen Letter	Provenience	Length	Width	Thickness	Weight	Lateral Cross Section	Longitudinal Cross Section	Left Edge Angle	Right Edge Angle	Nature of Defect Causing Rejection
h.	6.0N3.0W .55-.60	1.80	1.74	.41	1.5	Cvx	Cvx	41°-45°	27°-35°	Material flaw and step fracture during end-thinning
f.	6.0N4.5W .55-.60	2.10	2.77	.86	6.7	Plano	Plano	44°-46°	43°-46°	Material flaw
c.	6.0N6.0W .45-.50	1.60	.97	.35	.7	Cvx	Cvx	---	30°-35°	Overshot (?), hinge fracture
b.	6.0N6.0W .50-.55	3.27	1.15	.64	2.4	---	---	---	40°-55°	Overshot
d.	6.0N6.0W .55-.60	3.30	1.49	.72	3.8	Cvx	Cvx	45°-60°	45°-60°	Overshot with hinge fracture
g.	7.5N3.0W .80-.85	3.70	2.39	.72	4.7	Cvx	Plano	35°-45°	--	Hinge fracture caused by lateral thinning
i.	7.5N3.0W .85-.90	2.92	1.57	.60	2.3	Plano	Plano	---	35°-50°	Hinging during removal of overly large flakes
a.	7.5N4.5W .65-.70	1.22	3.11	.65	2.7	Cvx	Cvx	---	65°	Overshot, hinge fracture
j.	7.5N6.0W .55-.60	2.27	1.59	.98	1.6	Cvx	Plano	35°	35°	End-thinning overshot with hinge fracture
k.	7.5N9.0W .45-.50	1.77	2.13	.66	2.6	Cvx	Plano	50°	50°	End-thinning overshot with step fracture
e.	9.0N1.5W .90-.95	2.92	1.11	.13	2.1	Plano	Cvx	40°-60°	40°-60°	Hinge fracture, (overshot?)

TABLE 5. Metrical and Attribute Summary of Bifacial Rejects (Plate 5).

114

Specimen Letter	Provenience	Length	Width	Thickness	Weight	Lateral Cross Section	Longitudinal Cross Section	Edge Angle Left	Edge Angle Right	Nature of Defect Causing Rejection
a.	9.0N1.5W .70-.75 9.0N3.0W .80-.85 7.5N1.5W Band 3	3.71	6.25	1.45	37.0	Cvx Plano	Cvx Cvx	40°-50°	40°-50°	Longitudinal fracture evidenced by only half of striking platform and flake scar extant
b.	9.0N3.0W .80-.85	6.92	1.39	1.16	13.8	Plano Cvx	Plano Cvx	40°	40°	Longitudinal and step fractures
c.	9.0N7.5W .24 7.5N10.5W .10-.15	7.06	5.50	2.09	118.1	Plano Plano	Plano Plano	--	--	Step fracture on medial hump, material flaw

TABLE 6. Metrical and Attribute Summary of Core Remnants (Plate 6).

115

Specimen Letter	Provenience	Length	Width	Thickness	Weight	Longitudinal Cross Section	Lateral Cross Section	Edge Angle Left	Edge Angle Right	Comments
e.	7.5N3.0W .95	2.70	1.65	.35	1.5	Plano Plano	Plano Plano	40°-45°	45°-50°	
a.	7.5N3.0W 1.03	2.16	.88	.22	.6	Plano Plano	Plano Plano	50°-70°	37°-55°	BW: .88 BA: 50°
c.	7.5N6.0W .50-.55	2.49	.91	.23	.8	Cvx Plano	Cvx Cnv	65°-70°	40°-50°	BW: .82 FWD: .49 BA: 60° FLD: .89
d.	9.0N3.0W .55-.65	2.44	1.08	.25	1.0	Cvx Cvx	Plano Cnv	20°-24°	20°	
b.	9.0N3.0W .93/.95	5.96	3.14	.86	16.3	Cnv Cnv	Plano Plano	40°-55°	35°-45°	BW: 2.66 FWD: 1.55 FWV: 1.06 BA: 25° FLD: 3.70 FLV: 3.58

BA: (Basal Angle) edge angle at base
BW: (Basal Width) distance between ears at base
FLD: Length of flute on dorsal face

FLV: Length of flute on ventral face
FWD: Width of flute on dorsal face
FWV: Width of flute on ventral face

TABLE 7. Metrical and Attribute Summary of the Fluted Point and Miniature Points (Plate 7).

116

Specimen Letter	Provenience	Preparation	Striking Platform				Entire Specimen						Edge Angle Left	Edge Angle Right
			Lateral Length	Transverse Length	Bulb Thickness	Platform Angle	Length	Width	Thickness	Weight	Lateral Cross Section	Longitudinal Cross Section		
f.	6.0N4.5W .60-.65	--	--	--	--	--	3.31	1.83	.34	2.4	Cvx-Plano	Cvx-Plano	23°	21°
i.	6.0N6.0W .55-.60	Abr	.49	.15	.34	18°	2.23	1.18	.51	1.1	Cvx-Plano	Cvx-Plano	25°	27°
g.	6.0N6.0W .55-.60	--	--	--	--	--	2.20	1.72	.24	1.2	Cvx-Plano	Cvx-Plano	21°	22°
j.	6.0N6.0W .60-.65	Abr Trans	.62	.25	.25	26°	1.72	1.30	.25	.7	Cvx-Plano	Cvx-Plano	25°	25°
e.	6.0N6.0W .60-.65	--	--	--	--	--	2.23	1.63	.28	1.3	Cvx-Plano	Cvx-Plano	21°	21°
h.	6.0N7.5W .53	Abr Trans	.67	.22	.28	20°	2.97	1.42	.25	1.3	Cvx-Plano	Cvx-Cnv	21°	21°-24°
c..	7.5N4.5W .65-.70	--	--	--	--	--	1.51	1.68	.23	.8	Cvx-Plano	Cvx-Plano	21°-24°	22°
b.	7.5N4.5W .65-.70	--	--	--	--	--	1.98	1.88	.23	1.0	Plano-Plano	Plano-Plano	24°	22°-24°
k.	7.5N6.0W .50-.55	Abr Trans	1.13	.31	.17	40°	2.79	2.01	.40	2.6	Cvx-Plano	Cvx-Cnv	25°-30°	23°
a.	7.5N6.0W .50-.55 .60-.65	--	--	--	--	--	2.63	1.59	.31	1.7	Cvx-Plano	Cvx-Plano	23°-26°	23°-27°
d.	7.5N6.0W .55-.60	--	--	--	--	--	2.13	2.05	.27	1.5	Cvx-Plano	Plano-Plano	21°	21°

TABLE 8. Metrical and Attribute Summary of Unutilized Channel Flakes (Plate 8).

Specimen Letter	Provenience	Preparation	Lateral Length	Transverse Length	Bulb Thickness	Platform Angle	Length	Width	Thickness	Weight	Lateral Cross Section	Longitudinal Cross Section	Dorsal Angle	Ventral Angle	Type and Length of Utilization
a.	6.0N3.0W .70--.75	Lat	.51	.15	.33	30°	3.87	2.77	.51	3.1	Cvx / Plano	Cvx / Cnv	30°		E, .68(N)
d.	6.0N6.0W .35--.40	Trans	.85	.35	.47	22°	4.35	2.28	.35	4.1	Cvx / Plano	Cvx / Cnv	45°		E, .20(N)
c.	6.0N6.0W .56	--	--	--	.40	21°	3.75	3.03	.52	5.0	Cvx / Plano	Cvx / Cnv	20°-	35°	.95, 1.06(Ni) / 2.40, 2.07(N)
b.	6.0N6.0W .65--.70	Trans	1.45	.67	.75	30°	3.51	2.22	.51	3.7	--	Cvx / Cnv	20°-	23°	.47, 1.45 (Ni)
e.	6.0N6.0W .65--.70	Trans Abr	1.04	.24	.43	30°	4.19	2.53	.43	4.2	--	Cvx / Cnv	20°-	25°	E, .63(N)
1.	6.0N7.5W .45--.50	Trans	.91	.28	.27	64°	3.49	2.09	.20	2.1	Plano / Plano	Plano / Cnv	10°-	15°	1.25, 1.30 / 1.12, .97(N)
f.	7.5N6.0W .45--.50	Abr	.83	.28	.35	10°	2.26	1.29	.35	1.2	Cvx / Plano	Cvx	20°		1.08(N)
j.	7.5N7.5W .50--.55	--	--	--	--	--	3.18	2.67	.35	2.5	Cvx / Plano	Cvx / Plano	20°-	27°	1.45(N),

	Provenience										Cross-section		Angle	Comments
k.	7.5N7.5W .50-.55	Trans Abr	.77	.32	.26	40°	1.93	1.19	.27	.8	Cvx Plano	Cvx Plano	20°- 27°	.73, .78, .50(N), P
g.	7.5N7.5W .55-.60	Trans Abr	.93	.28	.64	20°	2.85	3.61	.63	6.8	Cvx Cvx	Cvx Plano	30°- 35°	3.10, .50, .50(N), P
h.	9.0N3.0W .90-.95	Abr	.53	.15	.26	15°	2.85	2.06	.30	1.8	Plano Cvx	Plano Plano	21°- 25°	3.10(N), P
i.	9.0N7.5W .45-.50	Crsh	.60	.23	.31	12°	3.11	2.11	.29	2.0	Plano Plano	Cvx Cnv	20°- 22°	E
		Utilized Channel Flakes												
d.	6.0N4.5W .61	--	--	--	--	--	2.76	1.55	.26	1.6	Plano Plano	Plano Plano	22°- 24°	E
c.	7.5N7.5W .55-.60	--	--	--	--	--	3.03	1.69	.26	1.6	Cvx Plano	Cvx Plano	20°	1.23(N)
b.	7.5N9.0W .45-.50	--	--	--	--	--	3.63	1.51	.25	1.7	Cvx Plano	Cvx Plano	20°	.37(N)
a.	9.0N6.0W .68	--	--	--	--	--	4.78	1.47	.25	2.3	Cvx Plano	Cvx Cnv	20°- 23°	E, .90(N) .87, .72, 1.17(Ni)

Crsh: Crushed E: Erratic nicking or nibbling N: Nibbled Ni: Nicks P: Polish

TABLE 9. Metrical and Attribute Summary of Utilized Flakes, including Utilized Channel Flakes (Plates 9, 10).

Specimen Letter	Provenience	Length	Width	Thickness	Weight	Longitudinal Cross Section	Lateral Cross Section	Retouched Edge Angle	Location of Retouch
a.	9.0N6.0W .15–.20	2.62	3.55	1.42	11.8	Cvx Plano	Cvx Plano	35°–47°	End
c.	9.0N7.5W .23	5.79	3.51	1.15	24.7	Cvx Plano	Cvx Cnv	40°–60°	Lateral
b.	Test Area 3 6–9"	1.34	1.26	.30	.9	Plano Plano	Plano Plano	50°–75°	Lateral, End

TABLE 10. Metrical and Attribute Summary of Scrapers (Plate 11).

120

Specimen Letter	Provenience	Preparation	Striking Platform				Entire Specimen								
			Lateral Length	Transverse Length	Bulb Thickness	Platform Angle	Length	Width	Thickness	Weight	Longitudinal Cross Section	Lateral Cross Section	Edge Angle Left	Edge Angle Right	Edge Angle on Tip(s)
d.	6.0N4.5W .60–.65	Trans Abr	.88	.22	.36	40°	3.78	3.09	.80	6.9	Cvx Plano	Cvx Cnv	70°–80°	70°–80°	Edges of tip: 70°
a.	6.0N9.0W .53		—	—	—	—	4.05	3.86	.13	12.2	Plano Plano	Plano Plano	55°–65°	65°	Edges of tip: 70°
e.	7.5N7.5W .50–.55	Lat Abr	.69	.27	.35	30°	2.37	2.05	.49	1.8	Cvx Plano	Cvx Cnv	70°–80°	70°–80°	Edges of tip: 70°
c.	7.5N7.5W .55–.60		—	—	—	—	.85	1.83	.36	.6	Plano Plano	Plano Plano	45°–50°	45°–50°	Edges of tip: 50°
b.	9.0N3.0W .85–.90	Lat	.35	.13	.18	22°	3.85	1.56	.25	1.7	Cvx Plano	Cvx Plano	55°–65°	65°	Edges of tip: 75°
DRILL															
f.	4.5N4.5W .60–.65		—	—	—	—	3.88	3.10	1.19	14.3	Cvx Cvx	Cvx Cnv			Between tips: 60° Base of broken tips: 65° – 70°

TABLE 11. Metrical and Attribute Summary of Gravers and Drill (Plate 12).

121

STRIKING PLATFORM | ENTIRE SPECIMEN

Specimen letter	Provenience	Preparation	Lateral Length	Transverse Length	Bulb Thickness	Platform Angle	Length	Width	Thickness	Weight	Lateral Cross Section	Longitudinal Cross Section	Edge Angle(s) of Spur	Edge Angle(s) of Retouch/Utilization	Location of Spur
e.	6.0N6.0W .45–.50	Trans	1.14	.37	.37	21°	3.14	2.89	.32	3.1	Plano Plano	Cvx Cnv	27°	32°–34°	Distal Right
a.	6.0N6.0W .45–.50	--					3.21	2.45	.15	1.3	Plano Plano	Cvx Cnv	34°–58°	58°	Distal Right
h.	6.0N9.0W .50–.55	--					3.67	2.61	.40	3.0	Cvx Plano	Cvx Cnv	27°–35°	22°–30°	Distal
j.	7.5N1.5W .84	Trans	.70	.20	.21	30°	1.65	1.34	.29	.5	Plano Cnv	Cvx Cnv	35°–60°	--	Right Lateral
f.	7.5N6.0W .65–.70	Lat	1.60	.54	.51	10°	3.01	2.41	.22	2.5	Cvx Plano	Plano Cvx	40°	35°	Right Lateral
l.	7.5N7.5W .45–.50	Abr	.53	.16	.46	30°	2.04	2.20	.20	1.8	Cvx Plano	Cvx Cnv	20°–70°	20°	Left Lateral
m.	7.5N7.5W .50–.55	--			None		.91	1.17	.09	.2	Plano Plano	Cvx Cnv	65°–75°	--	Proximal

EDGE WEAR (e.): Dorsal face from the midpoint of left lateral to spur to midpoint of right lateral. Spur tip is broken.

EDGE WEAR (a.): Distal end of dorsal face adjacent to spur.

EDGE WEAR (h.): Left lateral of dorsal face increasing in frequency towards the spur.

EDGE WEAR (j.): Major spur damage at tip.

EDGE WEAR (f.): Minor nibbling between spur and distal end on left lateral of dorsal face. Polish on medial ridge of spur. Impact fracture broke spur tip.

EDGE WEAR (l.): Minor nibbling on ventral face adjacent to 20° angle side of spur.

EDGE WEAR (m.): None

TABLE 12. Metrical and Attribute Summary of Graving Spurs (Plate 16).

	Measurements		Cross Section		Angle Range	Angle	Orientation	Edge Wear
g. 7.5N7.5W .55–.60	-- -- -- 1.53 2.75 .68 1.4		Cvx Plano	Cvx Cnv	30°–80°	30°	Left Lateral	Between spur and distal end on ventral face. Polish on medial ridge.
k. 7.5N7.5W .55–.60	-- -- -- 1.36 2.21 .24 .7		Cvx Plano	Cvx Plano	30°–50°	20°–50°	Left Lateral	Between spur and distal end of left lateral on ventral face. Broken spur tip.
d. 9.0N1.5W .90–.95	-- -- -- 3.18 2.51 .40 3.3		Cvx Cvx	Cvx Plano	20°–35°	35°	Distal	Distal end of dorsal face adjacent to spur. Spur tip broken. Impact fracture on medial ridge.
i. 9.0N3.0W .80–.85	-- -- -- 1.51 2.15 .35 .8		Cvx Plano	Cvx Cnv	40°		Left Lateral	None
c. 9.0N3.0W .80–.85	-- -- -- 2.58 1.98 .97 2.1		Cvx Plano	Cvx Cnv	45°–55°	20°–45°	Proximal Left	Some on right lateral of dorsal face. Minor spur tip break.
b. 9.0N3.0W .88	-- -- -- 2.17 3.18 .23 1.4		Plano Cvx	Plano Cnv	25°–50°	60°	Left Lateral	Between spur and striking platform on left lateral, and in central part of right lateral of dorsal face. Between distal end and midpoint of left lateral on ventral face. Ventral face of spur shows nibbling. Dorsal face has a scar from spur tip breaking.

123

Specimen Letter	Provenience	Striking Platform		Length	Width	Thickness	Weight	Entire Specimen		Utilized Edge Angle	Nature of Edge Wear
		Preparation	Platform Angle					Longitudinal Cross Section	Lateral Cross Section		
a.	7.5N1.5W .95	Trans	25°	5.28	5.32	2.30	65.6	Cvx	Cvx	40°–57°	Ni, N, P
b.	9.0N7.5W .13		——	5.59	3.20	.72	11.9	Cvx	Plano	32°–35°	P, N
SPOKESHAVE											
	6.0N3.0W .60–.65		——	5.00	3.92	1.47	19.6	Cvx	Plano	40°–55°	

TABLE 13. Metrical and Attribute Summary of Knives and Spokeshave (Plates 18, 19).

TABLE 14. Metrical and Attribute Summary of Retouched Flakes (Plate 20).

Specimen Letter	Provenience	Striking Platform					Entire Specimen							
		Preparation	Lateral Length	Transverse Length	Bulb Thickness	Platform Angle	Length	Width	Thickness	Weight	Lateral Cross Section	Longitudinal Cross Section	Retouched Edge Angle	Location of Retouch
a.	6.0N1.5W 1.00-1.05	Lat	--	.45	.99	11°	3.82	2.94	.60	6.6	Cvx	Plano	47°	Proximal
b.	6.0N3.0W .90-.95	Trans	1.60	.27	.24	10°	1.59	2.62	.30	1.3	Plano	Plano	23°	Dorsal R Lateral
											Plano	Cnv	63°	Ventral Proximal
c.	6.0N4.5W .50-.55	--	--	--	--	--	1.92	2.05	.61	3.1	Cnv	Plano	53°-	Erratically - both faces and laterals
											Cvx	Cvx	84°	
d.	9.0N6.0W .65-.70	Trans	.60	.24	.31	20°	1.33	3.01	.31	1.4	Cvx	Plano	64°	Dorsal L Lateral

HAMMERSTONE

Provenience					Length	Width	Thickness	Weight
6.0N3.0W .45-.50					7.35	5.60	4.99	275.7

BIFACIAL THINNING FLAKES

Specimen Letter	Provenience	Preparation	Lateral Length	Transverse Length	Bulb Thickness	Platform Angle	Length	Width	Thickness	Weight
c.	6.0N6.0W .50-.55	Trans Abr	.68	.30	.29	30°	3.24	1.47	.27	1.3
d.	6.0N6.0W .50-.55	Trans Abr	.92	.30	.26	30°	3.45	1.61	.24	1.3
b.	6.0N6.0W .60-.65	Trans Abr	1.45	.50	.44	46°	3.03	1.68	.37	1.9
a.	7.5N1.5W .85-.90	Trans Abr	1.04	.32	.33	55°	2.84	2.26	.30	1.7

TABLE 15. Metrical and Attribute Summary of Hammerstone and Bifacial Thinning Flakes (Plates 21, 22).

Total area excavated: 92.25m^2
Total area of Paleo-Indian component: 42.75m^2

Artifacts
    Debitage: 7360
        Flint: 7229
            Cortical: 12
            Bifacial Thinning Flakes: 253
            Heat treated/damaged: 32
        Quartz: 131
    Fluted Point: 1 (unfinished)
    Miniature Points: 4 (1, unfinished)
    Knives: 2 (probable)
    Cores: 3   (large bifacial rejects)
    Drill: 1   (two tips)
    Utilized Flakes: 16
    Retouched Flakes: 4
    Spurred Sidescraper: 1 (with a graver tip)
    Endscrapers: 1
    Sidescrapers: 2
    Channel Flakes: 15   (4, utilized)
    Bifacial Rejects: 12
    Gravers: 5
    Graving Spurs: 13
    Hammerstone: 1
    Spokeshaves: 2 (1, on a graver)

Carbon-14 date: 10,190 +/-300 years B.P.: 8240 B.C. (W3931)
Charcoal: Red oak, juniper or white cedar

TABLE 16.   Summary of Area Excavated, Artifacts, and
            Charcoal Date and Identification.

LEVEL

TABLE 17. Average (Mean) Weight for Flint Chips by Level for Each Square in the Paleo-Indian Component.

Square Number	1	2	3	4	5	6	7	8	9	10	11	12	13	All Levels
4.5N3.0W	.10													.10
4.5N4.5W	.50	.37	.83	.10	0	.20	.20							.46
6.0N1.5W	.15	.55	.20	.20		.10								.26
6.0N3.0W	.20	.20	.24	.24	.85	.10	.23							.32
6.0N4.5W	.23	.56	.45	.38	.38	.23	.38	.10		.20	0	.10	.20	.43
6.0N6.0W	.38	.49	.34	.35	.20	.20	.56	.20						.36
6.0N7.5W	.33	.25	.34	.29	.18	.20	.25	1.70	0					.28
6.0N9.0W	.50	.46	.21	.23	.18	.37	.33	.37	.23					.29
7.5N1.5W	.40	.34	.43	.31	.53	.26	.14	.21	.16	.80				.36
7.5N3.0W	0	.28	.29	.28	.28	.21	.37	.18	.30	.39				.29
7.5N4.5W	.31	.51	.34	.48	.53	.20	.78	.18	.20	.44	.20	.40	.15	.43
7.5N6.0W	.57	.28	.23	.19	.24	.16	.16	.23	.02	.35	0	.20		.27
7.5N7.5W	.27	.33	.41	.24	.20	.50	.30	.32						.32
7.5N9.0W	.26	.36	.19	.11	.10	.30	.90	.10						.29
9.0N1.5W	.57	.40	.34	.25	.22	.29	.40	.10	.45	.60				.39
9.0N3.0W	1.10	.30	.21	.42	.39		2.20	.27	.28	.10				.29
9.0N4.5W	1.10	.43	.58	.17	.20	1.24	.17	.10	.35		.61	.38		.48
9.0N6.0W	.31	.64	.76	.45		1.10	.30	.25	.31	0	1.44			.43
9.0N7.5W	.17	.44	.25	.11	.74	0	.33	.05	1.83	1.73	.20			.55
Square	.42	.33	.28	.27	.29	.26	.33	.24	.36	.63	.88	.33	.17	.31

Total weight/Total count

127

Square Number	Flint Count	Bifacial Count	FC Rank	BC Rank	FC–BC (D)	D²
4.5N4.5W	10	0	17	17.5	-.5	.25
6.0N1.5W	6	2	18	13.5	4.5	20.25
6.0N3.0W	36	2	16	13.5	2.5	6.25
6.0N4.5W	123	1	13	16	-3	9
6.0N6.0W	593	9	4	8	-4	16
6.0N7.5W	133	3	12	10.5	1.5	2.25
6.0N9.0W	176	0	9	17.5	8.5	72.25
7.5N1.5W	398	26	6	4	2	4
7.5N3.0W	868	28	2	3	-1	1
7.5N4.5W	263	12	7	7	0	0
7.5N6.0W	2466	86	1	1	0	0
7.5N7.5W	499	34	5	2	3	9
7.5N9.0W	175	7	10	9	1	1
9.0N1.5W	152	3	11	10.5	.5	.25
9.0N3.0W	725	23	3	5	-2	4
9.0N4.5W	49	2	15	13.5	1.5	2.25
9.0N6.0W	212	13	8	6	2	4
9.0N7.5W	94	2	14	13.5	1.5	2.25
						154.00

$$r_s = 1 - \frac{6(\Sigma D^2)}{N(N^2-1)} = 1 - \frac{(6)(154)}{18\,((18)(18)-1)} = .841$$

$$z = (r_s - 0)\,(\sqrt{N-1}) = (.8410732714)(\sqrt{17}) = 3.467$$

$$.5000000 - .499764 = (.0002326)(2) = .0004652$$
$$\text{(Blalock 1972: 558, Table C)}$$

TABLE 18. Rank Order Correlation for Occurrence of Flint Debitage and Bifacial Thinning Flakes (omitting 4.5N3.0W).

Square Number	Flint Count (X)	Bifacial Count (Y)	XY	X^2	Y^2
4.5N4.5W	10	0	0	100	0
6.0N1.5W	6	2	12	36	4
6.0N3.0W	36	2	72	1296	4
6.0N4.5W	123	1	123	15129	1
6.0N6.0W	593	9	5337	351649	81
6.0N7.5W	133	3	399	17689	9
6.0N9.0W	176	0	0	30976	0
7.5N1.5W	398	26	10348	158404	676
7.5N3.0W	865	28	24220	748225	784
7.5N4.5W	263	12	3156	69169	144
7.5N6.0W	2466	86	212076	6081156	7396
7.5N7.5W	499	34	16966	249001	1156
7.5N9.0W	175	7	1225	30625	49
9.0N1.5W	152	3	456	23104	9
9.0N3.0W	725	23	16675	525625	529
9.0N4.5W	49	2	98	2401	4
9.0N6.0W	212	13	2756	44944	169
9.0N7.5W	94	2	188	8836	4
Total	6975	253	294107	8358365	11019
(7.5N6.0W)	2466	86	212076	6081156	7396
	4509	167	82031	2277209	3623

$$r= \frac{N\Sigma XY - (\Sigma X)(\Sigma Y)}{\sqrt{(N\Sigma X^2 - (\Sigma X)^2)(N\Sigma Y^2 - (\Sigma Y)^2)}}$$

$$\frac{18(294107) - (6975)(253)}{\sqrt{(18(8358365) - (6975)(6975))}(18(11019) - (253)(253))} = .954$$

Omitting 7.5N6.0W

$$\frac{17(82031) - (4509)(167)}{\sqrt{(17(2277209) - (4509)(4509))}(17(3623) - (167)(167))} = .815$$

TABLE 19. Product-Moment Correlation Between Flint Debitage and Bifacial Thinning Flakes in 18 Excavation Units (omitting 4.5N3.0W and 7.5N6.0W).

Area Designation	Sq. Feet (Sq. Meters)	No. Artifacts	No. Chips	Artifacts/ Chips	Artifact/Sq. Ft. (Sq. Meter)	Chips/Sq. Ft. (Sq. Meter)
DEBERT total	10,600 (984.78)	3935	23,636	.17	.37 (3.99)	2.23 (24.00)
A	925 (85.93)	278	1823	.15	.30 (3.23)	1.97 (21.21)
B	600 (55.74)	218	897	.24	.36 (3.91)	1.49 (16.09)
C	1425 (132.39)	600	3208	.19	.42 (4.53)	2.25 (24.23)
D	1250 (116.13)	170	6010	.03	.14 (1.46)	4.81 (51.75)
E	325 (30.19)	12	267	.04	.03 (.40)	.82 (8.84)
F	2200 (204.38)	1014	4936	.21	.46 (4.96)	2.24 (24.15)
G	1450 (134.71)	648	2343	.28	.45 (4.81)	1.61 (17.39)
H	375 (34.83)	104	591	.18	.28 (2.99)	1.58 (16.96)
I	350 (32.52)	97	652	.15	.28 (2.98)	1.86 (20.05)
J	1200 (111.48)	658	2742	.24	.55 (5.90)	2.29 (24.59)
	500 (46.45)	136	167	.81	.27 (2.92)	.33 (3.60)

(Derived from MacDonald 1968:21; Figs. 8-17; Table 2)

6LF21	460.16 (42.75)	75	7360	.01	.16 (1.75)	15.99 (172.16)
Excluding non-utilized Channel Flakes and Bifacial Rejects		50	7360	.01	.11 (1.17)	15.99 (172.16)
WEST ATHENS HILL (Systematic collection in only 600 sq. ft. of Area B (Ritchie and Funk 1973:30)	600 (55.74)	315	10,408	.03	.53 (5.65)	17.34 (186.71)
TWIN FIELDS (Eisenberg 1978:150, 155)	2500 (232.26)	121	1036	.12	.05 (.52)	.41 (4.46)

TABLE 20. Comparison of 6LF21 to Debert, West Athens Hill, and Twin Fields: Area Excavated, Number of Artifacts and Chips, and Density of Artifacts and Chips.

Area Designation	Fluted Points	Bifacial Rejects	Drills	Esquillees Pieces	Endscrapers	Sidescrapers	Perforators	Gravers	Graving Spurs	Spokeshaves	Retouched Flakes	Utilized Flakes	Unknown	Miniature Points	Knives	Totals
A	3	2	1	41	121	11	--	6	--	1	49	32	11	--	--	278
B	2	2	--	34	62	5	--	5	--	1	14	84	9	--	--	218
C	17	17	--	77	224	22	--	4	--	4	102	102	31	--	--	600
D	18	18	2	13	28	6	--	3	--	3	11	45	23	--	--	170 (172)*
E	2	1	--	--	3	--	--	--	--	--	1	3	2	--	--	12
F	10	35	1	95	362	47	4	6	--	5	291	106	42	--	--	1004 (1014)*
G	11	21	--	144	216	43	1	5	--	3	138	43	23	--	--	648
H	--	1	--	22	40	2	--	1	--	--	27	9	2	--	--	104
I	5	4	--	19	43	1	--	--	--	--	17	7	1	--	--	97
J	27	19	2	103	233	61	1	7	--	1	103	14	21	--	--	592 (658)*
One	--	6	--	38	31	3	--	1	--	--	31	16	10	--	--	136
Total	95	126	6	586	1363	201	6	38	--	18	784	461	175	--	--	3859 (3935)*
6LF21	1	15	1	--	1	3	--	5	13	2	4	16	--	4	2	67**

*Totals for each area and for the entire site as given elsewhere in the text.

**The additional spokeshave is a concave section on a graver. Channel flakes have been omitted from the comparison since MacDonald did not separate them in his study.

TABLE 21. Comparison of Artifact Frequencies at Debert to 6LF21 (MacDonald 1968: 28, Tables 2,3 as translated from percentages to counts).

132

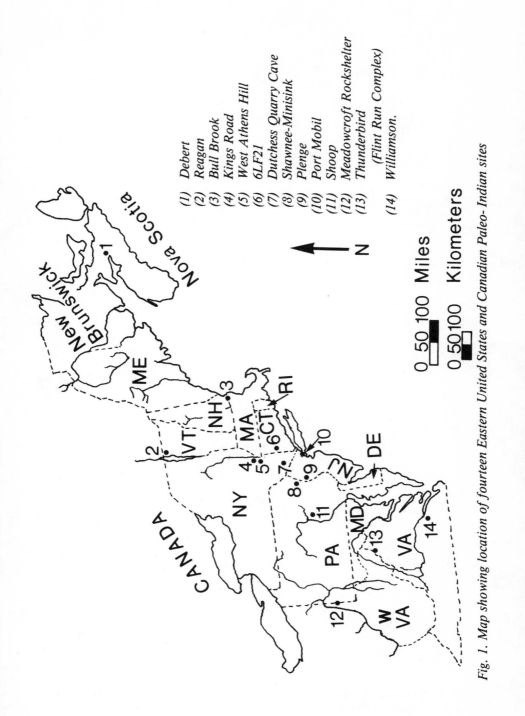

(1) Debert
(2) Reagan
(3) Bull Brook
(4) Kings Road
(5) West Athens Hill
(6) 6LF21
(7) Dutchess Quarry Cave
(8) Shawnee-Minisink
(9) Plenge
(10) Port Mobil
(11) Shoop
(12) Meadowcroft Rockshelter
(13) Thunderbird
     (Flint Run Complex)
(14) Williamson.

Fig. 1. Map showing location of fourteen Eastern United States and Canadian Paleo-Indian sites

133

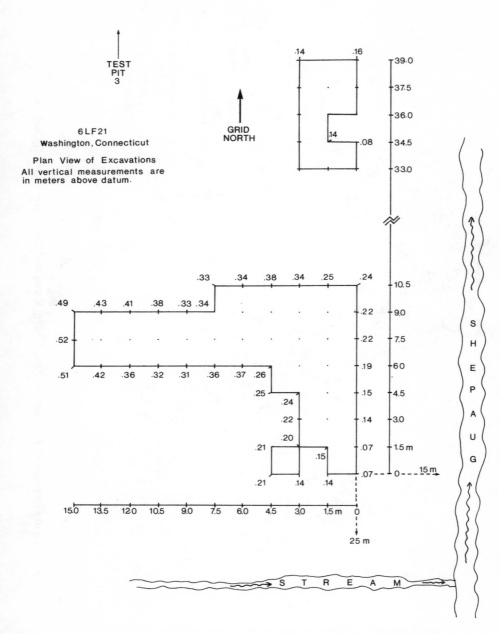

Fig. 2. Site plot showing location of excavation and Engelman's test pit #3,
Shepaug River, stream confluence, and relative elevations.

134

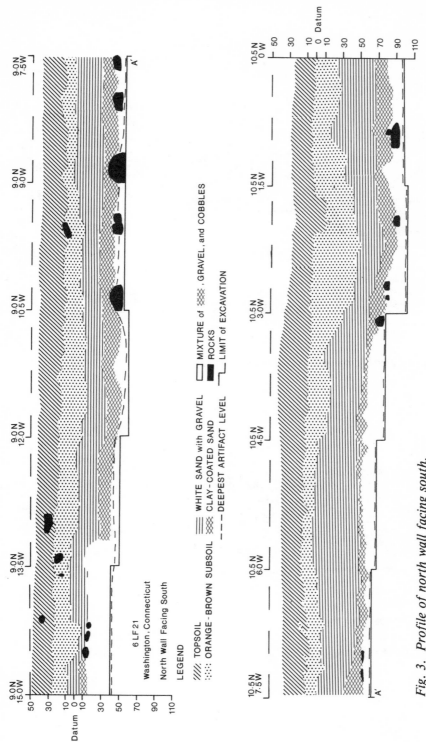

LEGEND

6 LF 21
Washington, Connecticut
North Wall Facing South

///// TOPSOIL
∷∷∷ ORANGE-BROWN SUBSOIL

≡≡≡ WHITE SAND with GRAVEL
∷∷∷ CLAY-COATED SAND

▨▨ MIXTURE of ▨▨, GRAVEL, and COBBLES
▪ ROCKS
⌐‾‾ LIMIT of EXCAVATION
– – – DEEPEST ARTIFACT LEVEL

Fig. 3. Profile of north wall facing south.

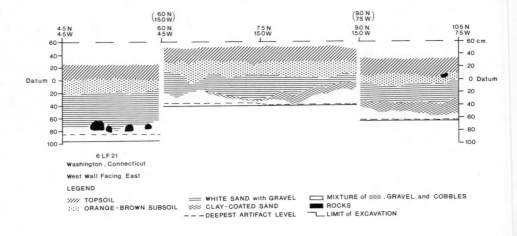

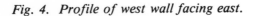

Fig. 4. Profile of west wall facing east.

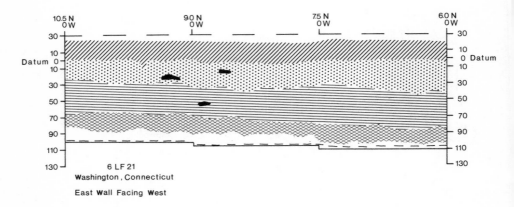

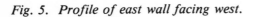

Fig. 5. Profile of east wall facing west.

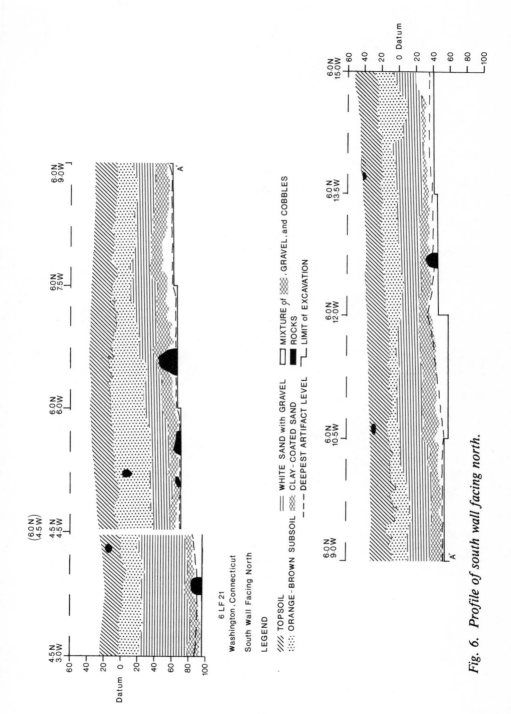

6 LF 21
Washington, Connecticut
South Wall Facing North

LEGEND

/// TOPSOIL
:::: ORANGE - BROWN SUBSOIL
≡ WHITE SAND with GRAVEL
▨ CLAY - COATED SAND
--- DEEPEST ARTIFACT LEVEL
▨ MIXTURE of ▨ GRAVEL, and COBBLES
■ ROCKS
⌐ LIMIT of EXCAVATION

Fig. 6. Profile of south wall facing north.

137

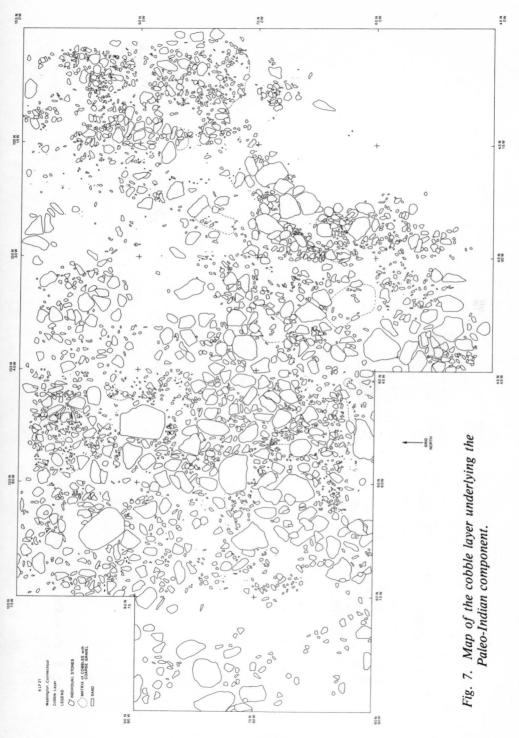

Fig. 7. Map of the cobble layer underlying the
Paleo-Indian component.

138

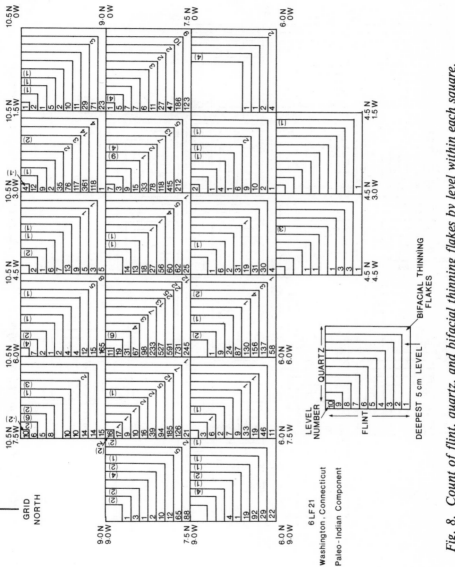

Fig. 8. *Count of flint, quartz, and bifacial thinning flakes by level within each square.*

139

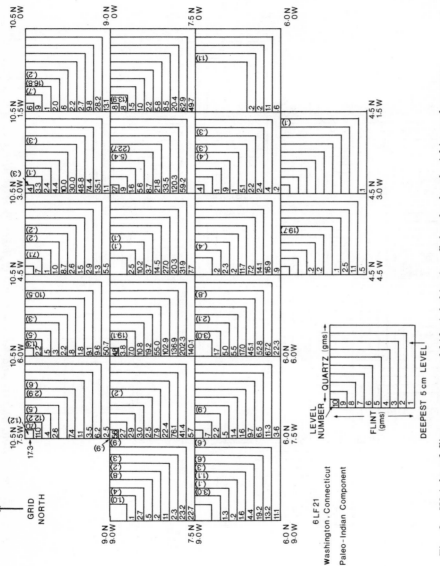

Fig. 9. Weight of flint, quartz, and bifacial thinning flakes by level within each square.

140

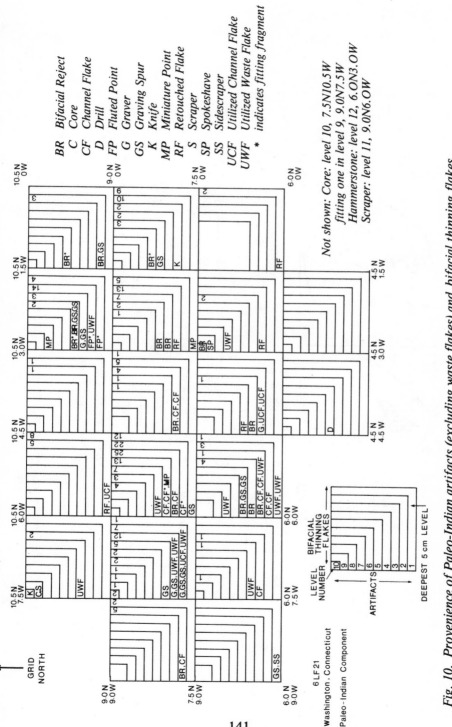

141

Fig. 10. Provenience of Paleo-Indian artifacts (excluding waste flakes) and bifacial thinning flakes.

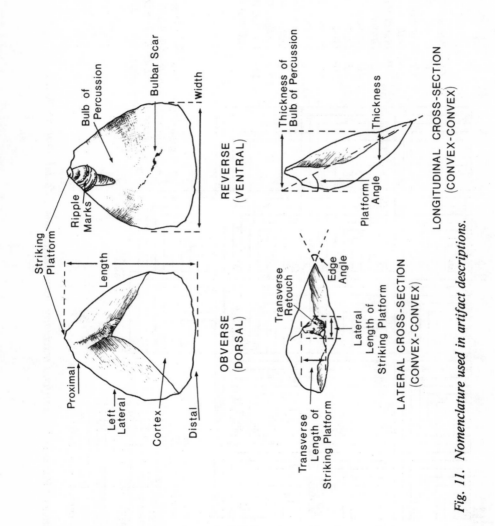

Fig. 11. Nomenclature used in artifact descriptions.

142

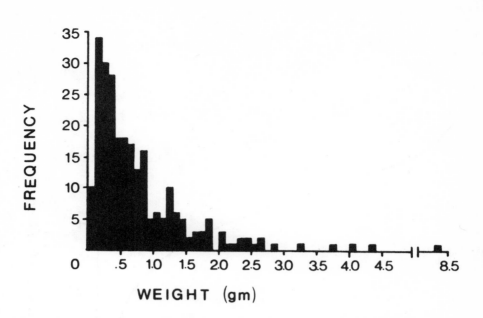

Fig. 12. Frequency distribution of bifacial thinning flakes by weight.

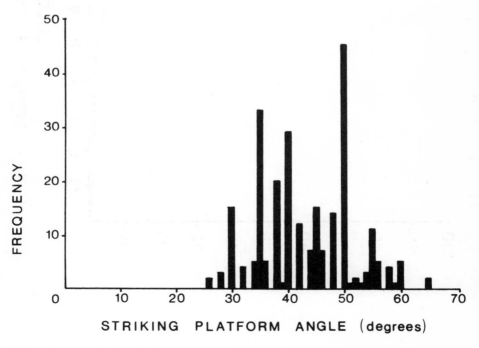

*Fig. 13. Frequency distribution of bifacial thinning flakes by striking plat-
form angle.*

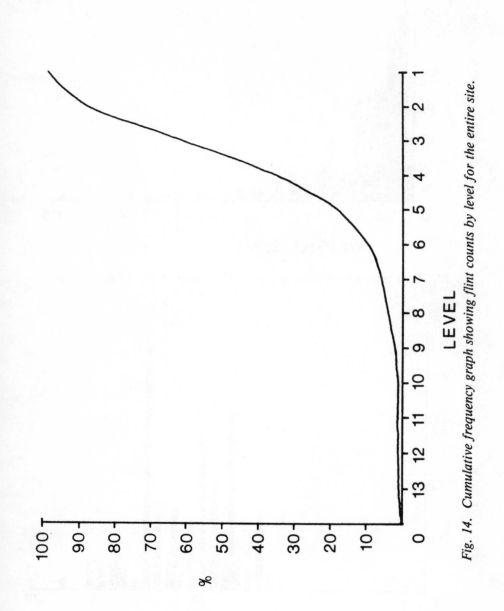

Fig. 14. Cumulative frequency graph showing flint counts by level for the entire site.

144

PLATE 1. Excavation in progress.

PLATE 2.   Cobble layer being mapped with aid of mapping frame.

PLATE 3.   *Wall profile being drawn to scale.*

147

PLATE 4.   View of cobble layer looking grid west.

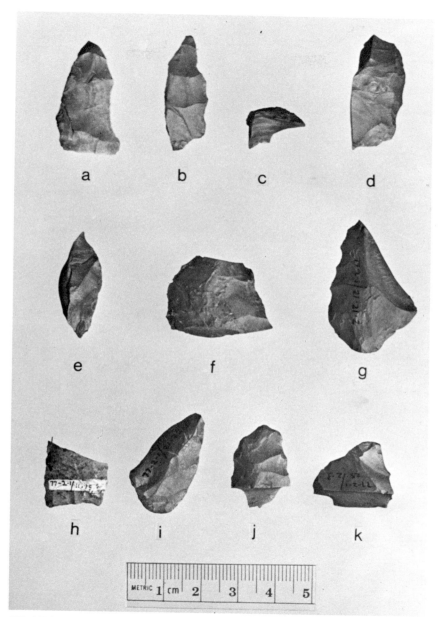

a   b   c   d

e   f   g

h   i   j   k

PLATE 5. Bifacial rejects.

PLATE 6.   Core remnants.

PLATE 7. *Fluted point, miniature points, and bifacially edged point.*

151

PLATE 8. Channel flakes.

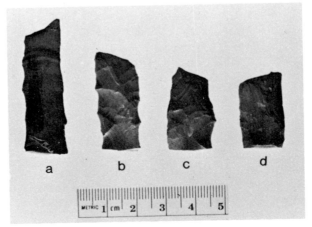

PLATE 9. Utilized channel flakes.

152

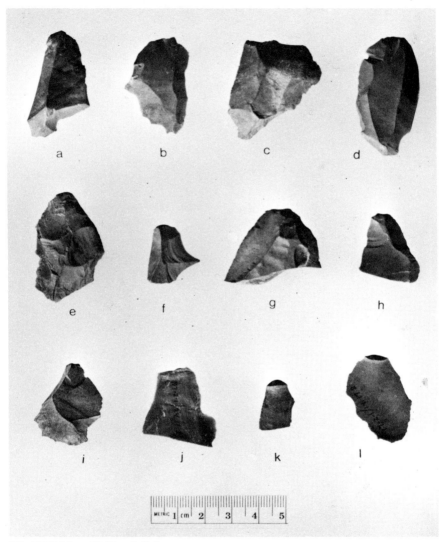

a   b   c   d

e   f   g   h

i   j   k   l

METRIC 1 cm 2 3 4 5

PLATE 10. Utilized flakes.

153

PLATE 11.   Scrapers.

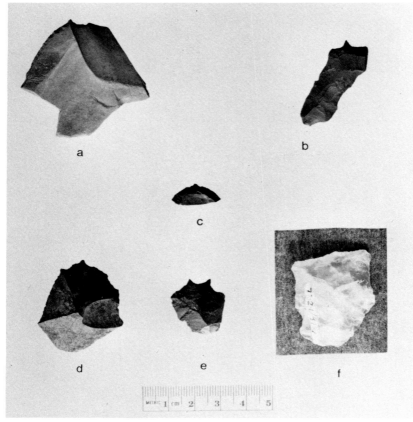

PLATE 12.   Gravers and drill.

154

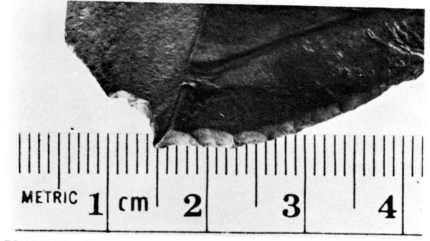

PLATE 13.   Close-up of graver.

PLATE 14.   Close-up of graver with spokeshave.

155

PLATE 15. Close-up of drill.

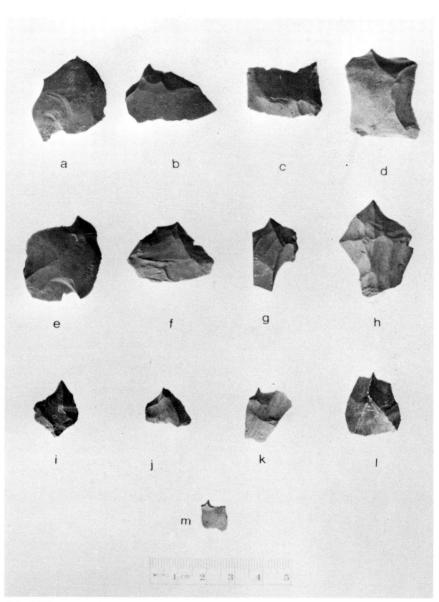

PLATE 16. Graving spurs.

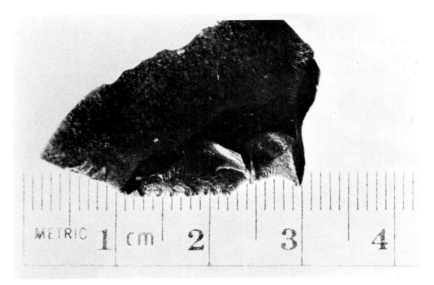

PLATE 17.   Close-up of graving spur.

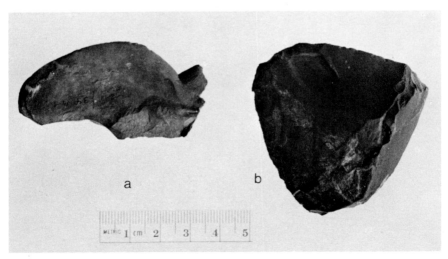

PLATE 18.   Knives.

158

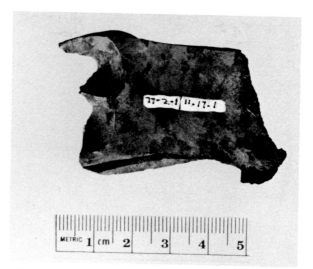

PLATE 19. Spokeshave.

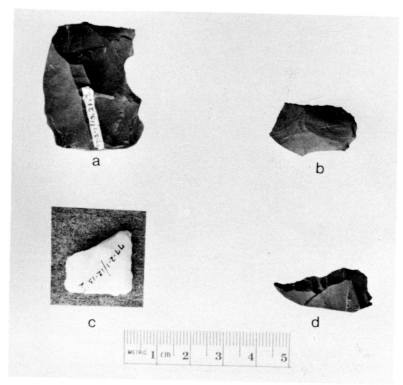

PLATE 20. Retouched flakes.

159

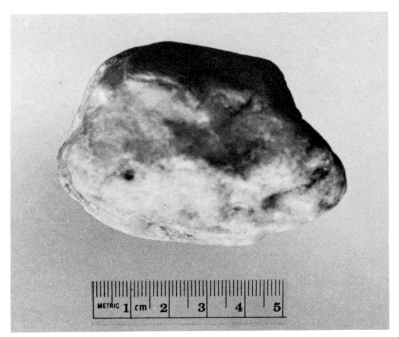

PLATE 21.   Hammerstone.

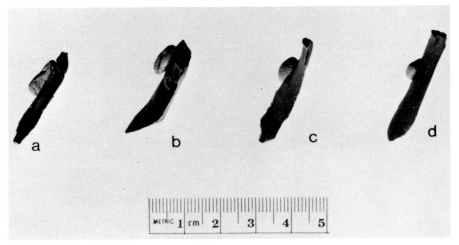

PLATE 22.   Bifacial thinning flakes.